Haroldo's approach to these devotions comes from seeing God in his everyday real-life work as a court interpreter in the Southern California Courts. Each vignette begins with the story of how individuals fare in court. There are triumphs but mostly sad, real-world experiences. He then "flips the script" as it were, and we are now in God's court or at least are looking at the human situation from a celestial Christocentric view. What is amazing is how each story turns just enough that you get a different look at another facet of God's love and grace. They take Romans 5:20 and give flesh to the skeletal statement "where sin abounded grace much more abounded". Even those of us grounded in grace will be pleasantly surprised at the increased breadth and depth of that grace illustrated in the stories.

Whether you read it as a devotional or just a read for encouragement you will have your view of the unfathomable richness and incomprehensible depth of our Savior's love for each of us.

Well worth every moment spent.

—Douglas L Bechard, MD

Dr. Camacho has done it again. In this, his second collection of reflections from his real-life experiences as a court interpreter, he has applied God's word to our real-life actions. Many people say that God's inspired word (the Bible) was given to an ancient people and has no place in our modern lives. But with his insightful reflections of real life today we see that God's word is very much for you and me today. God tells us "if you believe in what Jesus says and has done for each and every one of us" then for us ALL CHARGES HAVE BEEN DROPPED and we will dwell with Jesus in heaven forever. I recommend this devotional for all people of all ages.

—Craig Chaddock
Lay Minister, Our Savior Lutheran Church
(Plantation, Florida)

All Charges Dropped! Volume 2 has carried on the exquisite examples from Volume 1 of the daily trials suffered by guilty and innocent people alike. Dr. Haroldo S. Camacho opens the curtain for us to see how suffering and forgiveness can affect people's lives. I prefer the adoption and happy endings personally but realize not everyone's life is so blessed. These books are a wonderful addition to my daily devotions as each snippet from the courtroom is related to Bible truths. Thank you, Dr. Camacho, for opening your world for our enlightenment.

—Kim Schuh
Davie, Florida

Haroldo and I have been acquaintances, through a mutual friend, Carlos Perez, for many years. One day, on my lunch break, I was dining alone at a Chinese restaurant when Haroldo entered with his cohort of interpreters from the local courthouse. He didn't notice me, and I didn't want to bother him, so I just sat and ate my hot and sour soup and, with great interest, listened to this group of translators debate the meaning of one word for nearly half an hour. It was stunning to me to consider how much thought and care translators give to their craft.

With that said, understand this, ever since, by God's grace, Haroldo was set free from the condemnation of the law by the glorious gospel of Jesus Christ, he has been as equally passionate to share this good news with others. This book reflects that passion and goes to great lengths to comfort the reader with the message that, no matter who you are or what you have done to deserve God's wrath and condemnation, for the sake of Jesus, you are forgiven. This book is a fantastic resource for broken people everywhere.

—Kevin Hempe
Third-year Seminary Student
Concordia Theological Seminary, Fort Wayne, Indiana

ALL CHARGES DROPPED!

{ VOLUME 2 }

ALL CHARGES DROPPED!

{ VOLUME 2 }

Devotional Narratives from Earthly Courtrooms to the Throne of Grace

HAROLDO S. CAMACHO

Foreword by Donavon Riley

All Charges Dropped! Devotional Narratives from Earthly Courtrooms to the Throne of Grace, Volume 2

Published by:
1517 Publishing
PO Box 54032
Irvine, CA 92619-4032

Publisher's Cataloging-In-Publication Data
(Prepared by The Donohue Group, Inc.)

Names: Camacho, Haroldo S., author. | Riley, Donavon, writer of foreword.
Title: All charges dropped! : devotional narratives from Earthly courtrooms to the throne of grace. Volume 2 / by Haroldo S. Camacho ; foreword by Donavon Riley.
Description: Irvine, CA : 1517 Publishing, [2023] | Also published simultaneously in Spanish under title ¡Se retira la demanda! Relatos devocionales desde la corte terrenal hasta el trono de la gracia. | Includes bibliographical references.
Identifiers: ISBN: 978-1-956658-06-4 (paperback) | 978-1-956658-07-1 (ebook)
Subjects: LCSH: Christianity and law—Prayers and devotions. | Criminal justice, Administration of—Religious aspects—Christianity. | Trials—Religious aspects—Christianity. | Law (Theology)—Prayers and devotions. | God (Christianity)—Mercy. | Christian life. | LCGFT: Devotional literature. | BISAC: RELIGION / Christian Living / Devotional. | RELIGION / Christian Living / General. | RELIGION / Christian Theology / General.
Classification: LCC: BR115.L28 C36 2022 | DDC: 241.2—dc23

The devotional narratives were inspired by the author's experiences as a court translator. But any similarity to actual persons, living or dead, or actual events, is purely coincidental. Information about names, ages, gender, and location have been modified to protect any and all individuals who inspired the narratives. Any similarity to a specific person or case is purely coincidental.

No narrative is intended as legal advice and should not be taken as such. Neither are the specific references to the law to be considered as accurate representations of the law in any and all circumstances.

Printed in the United States of America.

Cover art by Zachariah James Stuef.

Dedication

To the congregation at Our Savior Lutheran Church (Plantation, FL) who so lovingly and unconditionally have welcomed us into their family.

Contents

Foreword

The apostle Paul's central thesis is that we cannot persist in relying on our own powers. Our condition, into which we are born, can never be anything but one of helplessness and conflict. As a consequence, there is only one way this can be halted. Jesus Christ must come to us.

This was Paul's experience, as we learn from his epistles. So long as Paul remained a Pharisee, even being the "Pharisee of Pharisees" as he claimed, he was trapped in a hopeless struggle. He knew as well as anyone God's commands and that he must live as a good and righteous man. But, despite his earnest desire to accomplish this, his efforts came to nothing.

Then Jesus Christ came to him. The God he prosecuted and persecuted revealed the truth to Paul, translating Paul into the kingdom of Christ and transforming and renewing the thoughts of his mind. Christ now ruled over Paul's life and the result was his old self was annihilated. Paul now differed in every way from the zealous Pharisee who clung to the law as a guide and goad for living a righteous life before God.

Paul underwent what so many, including the author of this book, have experienced: even when we live according to the tenets of God's commands and man's laws we are not strong enough to conquer our sinful hearts. As a consequence, we are reduced to pitiful creatures. Namely, that we recognize what we should do, and we genuinely want to do it, but we are incapable of sublimating our self-centeredness. In theological terms, that's what's meant by the Church's doctrine of original sin. We are sinners, which means we are inherently selfish and there's nothing we can do to reverse direction and become wholly selfless, as God demands of us. The tragedy of human existence then is that in our pursuit of a good and righteous life we become more and more selfish.

This book then, like St. Paul's epistles, has much to say about the old and new life; specifically how life and righteousness may be attained.

The only means for the attainment of life and righteousness is given by God as a free gift. Jesus Christ, not the law, accomplishes the impossible for us. Jesus' death and resurrection relieve us of the burden, the intolerable constraints of daily trying to live in such a way that we can prove ourselves worthy to stand before the living God and hear him say: Well done, good and faithful servant!

It is this radical proclamation that changes everything for us. Now there is no longer any talk of what we should do and leave undone. There is no longer any debate about obeying God's commands by exercising our willpower. Now that Christ is risen from the dead it is evident from the preaching of the Gospel and the administration of his gifts of salvation that only one principle is operative in the lives of Christians: the unforced, spontaneous love of God poured out upon us in abundance in and through Jesus Christ.

In this book then, the reader will discover evidence for Christ that demands no verdict. The author understands well that, despite the goodness of the law, it lays a terrible burden upon us. The law's demands that we live a good and righteous life drives us into troubles and perplexities, not because the law is pulling a bait and switch on us but because we are helpless to do what it commands. So, in a remarkably Pauline way, the author tells us this himself through a series of meditations taken from his own life, to relieve us of the terrible burden of the law, and comfort us with the Gospel of Jesus Christ. A Gospel that declares:

. . . at the right time, while we were still powerless, Christ died for the ungodly. Very rarely will anyone die for a righteous man, though for a good man someone might possibly dare to die. But God proves His love for us in this: While we were still sinners, Christ died for us (Romans 5:6-8).

In the Name + of Jesus,
Rev. Donavon L. Riley
July 18, 2022

Preface

For over twenty years I heard countless guilty verdicts, heightened by the blow of the judge's gavel. Every working day I served as a Certified Court Interpreter for the judicial system in the California courts. Sometimes we would hear over 100 criminal and civil matters in a single day! Some were minor traffic infractions, others misdemeanors, others were serious felonies. There were also countless divorce petitions, Stay-away orders, allegations of child abuse, and Juvenile Court matters. At the center of each allegation, there was a human being who at one time had been a newborn child, representing the innocence, curiosity, joy, and promise of human existence. Yet, years later here was that same person, accused of any one of many crimes: armed robbery, assault, murder, rape, and all types of sexual assault, physical and sexual abuse of minors, drug trafficking, breaking and entering, drunk driving, drug abuse of all kinds, white collar crime, the list was endless. The humanity of most defendants appeared to turn against others as helpless and hapless as themselves.

Courtroom appearances, from arraignments through pretrials, trials, and sentencing were all a grand display of humanity at its worst, and rarely, at its best. I also witnessed the judicial system at its best and worst. Justice after all is in the hands of imperfect people: judges, attorneys, clerks, and yes, even interpreters. Sometimes one was left to wonder if some judicial officers and other court officers were misguided by their own prejudices against the different, the stranger, the immigrant, and the helpless. But mostly, the law reigned. The law covers every minutia of criminal conduct and applies a corresponding punishment. But the written law is blind to tears of remorse, pleas for leniency, repentance, and promises of changed behavior. It seemed as if the unyielding nature of the law produced, at least in some, greater evil instead of repentance. I saw hearts grow colder and harder, in judges as well as in delinquents, under the suffocating demands of civil and criminal law.[1]

In this little book you will find many of those narratives. However, there is but only one abiding story, the story of the Gospel. The short stories told here serve only as a megaphone to tell the greatest story arising from God's own courtroom, dictating its own verdict of grace over humanity. It is the Good News of God's astonishing initiative in Jesus Christ handing down verdicts of absolution to guilty sinners, but at a great cost—the voluntary incarnation of God's only Son, Jesus Christ. He became our substitute in his life, death, and resurrection. Through Christ's completed work, God was able to dictate grace instead of condemnation, forgiveness instead of sentencing to guilty sinners, entirely through God's grace in Christ alone, and by faith alone. Each narrative moves from the unyielding dictates of human law to the courtroom before the presence of God, where the law is even more unbending. That is why Jesus Christ voluntarily became flesh so that the full weight of God's law would fall upon him. That way sinners receive grace and mercy through the life and sacrifice of Christ.

Some may see too much grace in the gospel story as told here, and I sincerely hope that is the case. Paraphrasing Luther's Preface to his Commentary on Galatians, "I formulated these narratives only for the perturbed, the afflicted, the tempted (the only ones who can understand such grace), those who are despondent in their faith. Those who need more instruction on how to live a pious life, might as well go to other books, with better narratives of self-improvement, and proven steps for defeating evil in all aspects of life, for they are legion."[2]

My gratitude to Mercedes, my wife, the prime motivator encouraging me to put these stories in writing, Thanks also to my

---

[1] Any similarity to actual persons, living or dead, or actual events, is purely coincidental. Specific identifying marks such as names, ages, at times gender, have been modified/edited to protect any and all individuals referenced. Any similarity to a specific person, persons, or case, is purely coincidental.

[2] *Martin Luther's Commentary on Saint Paul's Epistle to the Galatians (1535)*, xix. Translated by Haroldo Camacho, 1517 Publishing, 2018.

eleven-year-old son, Orlando, who daily teaches me what it means to issue and receive our own daily verdicts of forgiveness. But this little book is for you, the reader. Make it yours. Draw on it, highlight it, read it alone or with loved ones every day, memorize Bible texts that jump out at you, copy them by hand, put them on your digital screens, tweet them, make them your own comfort. For God's verdict over you, the guilty one, has pounded a booming "Not Guilty" decree! All charges have been dropped. Your record is clean. Christ has taken your place in life and death, and so, "You are *eternally* forgiven."

January 22, 2022
Davie, Florida

1

Under What Bridge Am I Going To Live With My Kids?

> "Jesus said to him: I am the way, the truth, and the life . . ." (John 14:6 ESV).

"And, where would you like me to go with my five children? Under a bridge?" This single father was responding to his attorney. The owner of the apartment was suing with an eviction notice, because he was in default with the rent and had not left the premises. "You have until the end of the month to find a place."

"And where do you suggest I go live with my kids, under a bridge?" he responded angrily and sarcastically.

"You have to leave the premises. The problem is that you signed the rental agreement with a false identity. You lied in order to get into those low housing rentals. You must promise the judge you will leave before the end of the month, yes or no?"

"That's totally unfair," he retorted. "The children's school is nearby, and the lady who takes care of them when I work is just down the street. I now have my own ID. I'll even pay more rent than he's asking! Let the judge know, please."

"Then let's go before the judge, and she'll decide."

The judge did not hear all the arguments. "The law is clear. You must vacate the premises immediately. You had until the end of the month; now you must leave in three days!" ruled the judge.

The man left with his chin on his chest. I walked out with him to offer at least sympathy and comfort. "So you really have nowhere to go?" I asked.

"No," he affirmed. "I'm totally alone in this country."

"And what about the children's mother?" I inquired.

"She abandoned us over a year ago. I'm totally alone, no one to turn to." We were in the hallway. Just then, the ladies' bathroom door opened and out walked a well-dressed, elegant looking woman about the man's age, who did not hesitate to kiss him tenderly on the lips. "So, how did it go, my love, are you ok?" she asked. He totally ignored me as he took her hand. As they walked out of the courthouse, she then tucked her arm under his. I was left speechless.

But he who is free from lies and deceit, let him cast the first stone. Who has not exaggerated his achievements just a tad over the truth? Or, what about that pretext we gave when we got to work late? Sometimes even with a look, a gesture, or even our silence we distort the truth for our convenience. Only of Jesus Christ has it been truly said, "no deceit was found in his mouth" (1 Peter 2:22, EHV). Also, Scripture states of him only that he was "holy, innocent, pure, separated from sinners, and exalted above the heavens" (Hebrews 7:26, EHV). He himself gave witness of his integrity saying, I am the "truth and the life" (John 14:6, ESV), meaning that his life and truth are one and the same thing. But he did not come to make a show of his integrity, but to give it away. To whoever thinks he or she is the greatest liar in the world, he says, "I will substitute your lie and your evil with my truth and my life." Otherwise, your lies will find you out in the day of judgment. Thus, on the cross Jesus took upon himself all the lies of all the liars (that means every human being) throughout the history of humanity. In other words, he took on himself – who is the truth – the tyranny of falsehood. There on the cross, the one whose integrity alone was faultless, became the worst of all liars so that they would be considered full of honesty and truth. That includes you and me. Yet, the truth at the core of his being overpowered all falsehood—as proven by his resurrection.

In the story of our homeless liar, his lies were uncovered by the affections of the woman in the hallway. It was evident he had lied to the judge. Was she also complicit in his lies? It wasn't clear. But he certainly was not alone. So, what is better: to have company in a life of lies, or to be alone in a life of truth?

But Jesus does not meet us in our "life of truth." He meets us in our life of lies, in our falsehoods, in the untruth of our being, and in the company we create to cover up our nakedness. He meets us as a Comforter and not as a Moses along our slippery paths, and whispers where no one else can whisper, "I am the way, the truth, and the life" (John 14:6, ESV). And in the lonely hallways of life, he surprises us with the kiss of grace.

2

Returning Good For Evil?

> "For I am convinced that neither death nor life, neither angels nor rulers, neither things present nor things to come, nor powerful forces, neither height nor depth, nor anything else in creation, will be able to separate us from the love of God in Christ Jesus our Lord" (Romans 8:38-39, NIV).

"I scratched his face because my girlfriends were texting me, saying he was cheating on me, not just with one but several girls."

The defendant was explaining to her public defender what had happened; I translated the interview. "He had gone to live with his mom, so I went to see him 'cause I needed money for the baby's diapers. When I got there, he was sitting on the sofa. He had a couple of girls sitting on his lap, and one stood behind him giving him a massage. When he saw me, he shouted a bunch of obscenities, and they all laughed at me. Then he gets up and comes and hugs me. That's when I scratched his face. One of the girls called the police. They arrested both of us. They found drugs in his pockets. They let me go after a couple of days; he was let go after a week. But I'm going to defend myself against these assault charges."

"And, are you still living together?" asked the lawyer.

"No, he's still living in his mother's house. But a week ago, somebody ran a stop sign and crashed into him. He broke several ribs, a leg, and injured his head. I take him food every day and change his dressings because his mom won't take care of him."

"So, are you going to get back together again?" inquired the attorney.

"Well," she answered with a timid smile, "we're working on it."

You'll be the judge if she did right or wrong in caring for him, or even thinking of getting back with him. But in the insanity of her love for this unfaithful, perverse, and obscene human being, she was being true to Scriptures. "Do not repay anyone evil for evil . . . If your enemy is hungry, feed him; if he is thirsty, give him something to drink. In doing this, you will heap burning coals on his head" (Romans 12:17, 21, NIV).

But surpassing by far any human example is the reality of the work done by Jesus for us. He overcame our evil with his good. Ever since that first baby cry in Bethlehem we have ignored, resisted, fought, spurned his good with our evil. We denied him a place at the inn, placed him in a foul-smelling stable for a maternity ward, sought his death soon after his birth, sent him as a migrant to another country, opposed his teachings, arrested him under false pretenses, scratched his face with a crown of thorns, nailed him to a cross, and finally put him inside a cave and covered it with a huge stone. That was our evil, humanity's evil. In return, he lived a holy life in our place, resisted the fiercest temptations on our behalf, took our sin on the cross, buried our sins eternally with him, and resurrected as the promise of our resurrection. He returned all his good for all our evil, and with those stripes suffered by his good, healed our evil. "For I am convinced that neither death nor life, neither angels nor rulers, neither things present nor things to come, nor powerful forces, neither height nor depth, nor anything else in creation, will be able to separate us from the love of God in Christ Jesus our Lord" (Romans 8:38-39, NIV).

3

You're Going To Leave In A Body Bag

> "Those who are well have no need of a physician, but those who are sick; I came not to call the righteous, but sinners" (Mark 2:17, ESV).

When I looked at the file, I was taken aback: "Murder in the first degree." Moments later, during the interview with the lawyer, I realized the desperate situation of the accused. He had no witnesses in his favor; all the evidence was against him. He was alone in the country. He had found some sense of belonging by joining a gang. But they had a high entry price: he had to "erase" the leader of an opposing gang. It wasn't just any gang. It was a powerful criminal group operating in all the Americas. The young man saw a future in the gang. They offered him power, money, women. But first, he had to take a life. He would come in with some rank given the high profile of the target. He bought on. He stalked his victim and took him down with one shot. What he didn't know is that his handlers had set him up. They didn't want their own gang tagged with the crime. They just needed a hit man. But fooled by his own ambition, he felt into their trap. So, the gang itself snitched on him to the police. Now he was facing the death penalty. I had to translate the attorney's cold, cruel, but honest words: "Most likely, you'll leave prison in a body bag."

After a long pause, the defendant moaned, "Defend me until the end; I won't accept defeat."

It's difficult to defend lost causes. The lawyer has to either paint the picture with the starkest reality or use a palette of false hopes. Our heavenly attorney does not paint us any picture. He becomes our own reality; he takes on our own history. He became the criminal in our place. He felt the loneliness of helplessness. At Gethsemane, and then on the cross, he felt the death penalty overpowering his holy and innocent spirit. He suffered that capital punishment, which we deserved. His funeral shrouds formed his body bag. But he did not accept defeat. He is the only attorney who took the place of all his defendants and fought for them until the end, until he was satisfied with the work done, and exclaimed, "it is finished." But the shrouds could not contain him because "in him was life, and the life was the light of men . . . and the darkness has not overcome it" (John 1:4-5, ESV). He emerged from the tomb, ascended to the heavens, and from there, he'll return for the living and the dead. With his life, he defends you until the end, which will only be your true beginning. You will not be defeated. His life takes the place of your entire life. He is your birth, your death, your punishment, your future—all your life is hidden in him. "God gave us eternal life; and this life is in his Son" (1 John 5:11, ESV). Your future is not in a body bag. Your past, present, and future is the wrapping of his robe of righteousness, which covers every instant of your life. Does it seem strange that God extends such grace to criminals and sinners? Our Lawyer said, "Those who are well have no need of a physician, but those who are sick; I came not to call the righteous, but sinners" (Mark 2:17, ESV). Jesus Christ offers his defense work freely. He already has defended you until the end, which is only the portal to your new beginning, through which we have already entered, by his faith alone. "For you have died, and your life is hidden with Christ in God. When Christ who is your life appears, then you also will appear with him in glory." (Colossians 3:3-4, ESV). Yes, we moan, but it's that moan of faith that whispers, "Your will be done, wrap me in your salvation, hide my life in the life of Christ!"

4

The Tamal Cartel

> "For my flesh is real food, and my blood is real drink. Whoever eats my flesh and drinks my blood remains in me, and I in them" (John 6:55-56, NIV).

It's no joke. In fact, it should read "The Tamales Cartels," in the plural. Two adult twin sisters showed up at family court, each one requesting a Stay-Away Order from the other. But instead of the usual bond of care and understanding between twins, these two had a long history of quarrels, bickering, and competitive behavior. Finding themselves married and in a new country, they each started a little business making and selling tamales. They would park in strategic places at the entrance of grocery stores and other shopping centers with a large clientele interested in tamales. They competed for the best places to station themselves and offer their tasty goods.

On a certain day, one of them was standing at a strategic parking spot waiting for her husband to arrive, park, and sell her tamales from large pots in the trunk of the car. That's when her twin sister arrived in her car and proceeded to park in the other's guarded spot, slowly threatening to push her away with her car. A passerby pulled her away from danger while the other twin triumphantly emerged from her car to sell her wares. Convinced her sister had wanted to run her over, she called the police. The sheriffs, in turn, warned that if the sisters did not leave immediately, they would arrest them both. Now weeks later, they were each seeking relief from the judge to order the other to stay away. There was some muted laughter in the courtroom as each presented her arguments. But the judge's reaction was not funny. "If you are going to bring something before the court, bring something better than your tamales! Here we don't hear territorial disputes over Tamales Cartels! You both are grown women and should know better! Offer your tamales, but don't spice them up with your foolish quarrels. Both Stay-away orders are denied!"

Sacred history tells of history's first brothers: Cain and Abel. God had requested a sin offering. Cain was a tiller of the land, so he brought the best fruits of his harvest, beautiful fruits and vegetables, all truly organic. Abel was a shepherd, and so he brought a little lamb and sacrificed it before God's presence. The Biblical narrative says, "The Lord looked with favor on Abel and his offering, but on Cain and his offering he did not look with favor. So Cain was very angery, and his face was downcast" (Genesis 4:4-5, NIV). Soon after, Cain rose up against his brother and simply killed him! That was the beginning of religious wars throughout history, with senseless loss of life and extended hatred for generations. All for the same reason: What offerings do we bring before God for our sins? The best works of our hands? (Our tamales.) Or, the sacrifice of God's perfect Son, the Lamb of God that takes away the sin of the world. The Lord told us that his body is for us "real food, and my blood is real drink. Whoever eats my flesh and drinks my blood remains in my, and I in him" (John 6:55-56, NIV). His work was to bear on his own body our guilt and sins, and spill his blood for our forgiveness. And that is bread for our life, and life-giving drink. Above all, it is free, and is ours by grace through faith alone. Moreover, to eat and drink his life envelops us in love between brothers and sisters. "How good and pleasant it is when brothers live together in unity!" (Psalm 133:1, NIV).

5

An Unrepayable Debt

> "You were spiritually dead because of your sins and because you were not free from the power of your sinful self. But God made you alive with Christ. And God forgave all our sins" (Colossians 2:13, ERV).

"Lady, have you been making your monthly payments?" asked the lawyer.

"Yes, I haven't missed any, fifty dollars a month," she answered somewhat defensively.

"Do you have any idea of the balance?" continued the attorney.

"No, but I've got all the receipts here; I've already made fifteen payments." I was translating the interview.

"That's fine then. I'm going to show them to the district attorney. There's a chance she'll reduce the charges. For now, you are being accused of fraud to the Department of Social Welfare for over $25,000 dollars. Due to your immigration status in this country, you are not allowed to receive Social Welfare," the attorney quickly covered the facts of the case.

"Yes, I know I made a huge mistake. But when the police showed up at my house at four in the morning and arrested me in front of all my children, and dragged me to the police station, that was so humiliating. I am a single mother with five children. I work my fingernails off working in the fields. You have no idea of all the work it takes me to make those fifty dollars for the payment," she voiced her complaint.

But the lawyer continued. "Listen, the district attorney is making you an offer. If you promise today to pay the whole amount, the charges will be reduced to a simple misdemeanor. You will still have forty-five days of community service, and an extra $600 fee on top of what you owe. Further, because it's a misdemeanor, there's less of chance immigration will find out and deport you. Understood? Want to take the offer?"

"Well, I don't have many other choices, right?" At that point, the lawyer took out her calculator and punched in the numbers. That would be 505 monthly payments of fifty dollars each. At that rate it would take her forty-two years to pay off the debt. She was thirty-five years old. She would pay off her debt when she turned seventy-seven!

Jesus told the story of two debtors. One owed the king the equivalent of $10,000 dollars. Since he could not pay, the king decided to sell him, his wife, children, and all his goods to pay off the debt. But the servant pleaded his case, promising to pay the whole amount. Out of pure mercy, the king cancelled his entire debt. He would not accept small payments; he did not make such an offer. The debt could not be paid off in installments. It was either pay the whole amount, or accept forgiveness for the whole debt. He was simply F O R G I V E N. He was instantly freed from that entire burden.

But this same servant had a friend, a co-worker who owed him $200 dollars. Since he had not paid him, he sued him and sent him to jail. When the judge was told of the forgiven servant's cruelty toward his co-worker, he sent him to jail until he paid up every cent (Matthew 18:23-25). The king's mercy is astounding, but the forgiven debtor's cruelty leaves us speechless. But Jesus did not tell the whole story at that time. The rest of the story was told when he gave himself up to the cross. There he paid our other debt: the unfathomable depths of our cruelty against our neighbor. "You were spiritually dead because of your sins and because you were not free from the power of your sinful self. But God made you alive with Christ. And God forgave all our sins" (Colossians 2:13, ERV). Many disdain this dumbfounding gift of grace and prefer to put their trust in their daily payments of works, of working off their debt of sins, one effort of their will after another to transform their lives. They believe that with the accumulation of their payments, God will declare their sins forgiven at the end of their lives. But it will be an entire life of worthless payments, for they will all be declared null and void. For it is faith alone that grasps what is put in their hands, and that is the entire life of Christ put to their account. And it must be that life alone. Even if the smallest payment of works is mixed in with the gift of grace, everything will be rejected. "Now to the one who works, wages are not credited as a gift but as an obligation . . . And if by grace, then it cannot be based on works; if it were, grace would no longer be grace" (Romans 4:4, 11:6, NIV).

Otherwise, it's time to pull out the calculator. Punch in your debt of sins, plus the debt of your sinful nature. It's that nature that you cannot control: your anger, fury, lust, and thoughts of revenge against someone who has done you not the greatest but the least harm. Or your thoughts congratulating yourself for your advances and achievements against your sinful nature—those congratulatory thoughts are also evidence of your sinful nature. So, what's the total? How many installments would you need to make? How many lifetimes? How many eternities?

But "to the one who does not work but believes in him who justifies the ungodly, his faith is counted as righteousness" (Romans 4:5, ESV). Instantly. Faster than the speed of light, your debt is completely canceled, and you are declared eternally righteous before God. Instead of an eternity of payments, it's an eternity of grateful worship "To him who loves us and has set us free from our sins" (Revelation 1:5, CSB).

6

Where There's Smoke, There's Fire

> "Blessed is the man who walks not in the counsel of the wicked, nor stands in the way of sinners, nor sits in the seat of scoffers; but his delight is in the law of the LORD, and on his law he meditates day and night. He is like a tree planted by streams of water that yields its fruit in its season, and its leaf does not wither. In all that he does, he prospers" (Psalm 1:1-3, ESV).

When the defendant came before the judge, I could not help seeing the pictures he set out on the stand. I immediately knew he was about to get into worse problems. As a court interpreter, I am not allowed to advise the defendants on what they should say, or what evidence to present on their behalf. I am merely their voice in the English language. I am also the judge's voice in Spanish. The prosecution in this case was the Fire Department. The captain testified that the defendant had lit a bonfire in violation of the fire code for a residential zone. From his window at the station, the fire captain had seen a column of smoke rising from a housing complex. Although he had not received an emergency call, the fire captain had worried because "where there's smoke, there's fire." Immediately, he left for the area in a fire truck. When he arrived at the residence, he found two men placing branches from a recently pruned tree over some hot coals in a dug-out fire pit. But when the defendant testified, he insisted the pit had been only for a family barbecue. He said they just put the branches over the coals because "it was just easier to burn them than to haul them away;" but the pit posed no danger to them or to the nearby houses. As proof of his innocence, he brought pictures of the pit, smoking red-hot coals, included. "Look at the pictures for yourself, Your Honor, and you'll see that it was really nothing." The captain refuted the argument, saying that any fire pit, no matter how small, posed a danger in a residential zone, due to its flying embers. Since the defendant insisted, the judge finally took a look at the pictures. A brief smile crossed his face while he ruled, "The defendant is guilty of violating the fire code. He's ordered to pay the fine."

Many appear before God protesting their innocence. As proof, they bring their many works seeking to win God's approval. But where there's smoke, there's fire. God is a consuming fire, and those works are nothing but smoke in his nostrils (Isaiah 65:5). Those works do nothing but condemn us! Why? Because they are imperfect, defective, always tainted with some degree of self-interest, of the vain pleasure we feel when we are congratulated for them. Or perhaps because others look at us with greater respect than before, thinking we are more than we really are. Then there are so many more works we fail to do for ourselves and for others. Remember, the rule is to love our neighbor as ourselves. And do we really do this honestly, consistently, expecting nothing in return, not even recriminating someone for not noticing, or at least giving us a much-needed pat on the back?

On the other hand, neither can we come before him with works of disobedience, with evil works, with works of the flesh, or with works that evidence anger at ourselves and our neighbor, even in the slightest degree. These condemn us just the same.

Then, what proof are we to bring before our Judge? We can only offer the works of Christ, the only One whose heart was right, without spot, or blemish, whose love was entirely pure, without the slightest tinge of self-interest. Because the Judge of the Universe only recognizes those works as righteous, as acceptable in his sight. All other works, no matter how righteous, good, and worthwhile – and indeed many are all of this and more – are nonetheless rejected as filthy rags. "Indeed, it is by grace you have been saved, through faith—and this is not from yourselves, it is the gift of God—not by works, so that no one can boast" (Ephesians 2:8-9, EHV). The only picture God wants to see as evidence of your righteousness is that of Christ's. Any other face on that photo is self-incriminating of violating every moral code. Can't find a picture of Christ? Here's a word picture you can use: "Blessed is the man who walks not in the counsel of the wicked, nor stands in the way of sinners, nor sits in the seat of scoffers; but his delight is in the law of the LORD, and on his law he meditates day and night. He is like a tree planted by streams of water that yields its fruit in its season, and its leaf does not wither. In all that he does, he prospers" (Psalm 1:1-3, ESV). With his life he blows the smoke away, and then, when there's no smoke, there's no fire.

7

So, Who Else Is Lying?

> "The tax collector stood at a distance and would not even lift his eyes up to heaven, but was beating his chest and saying, 'God, be merciful to me, a sinner!" (Luke 18:13, EHV). Jesus concluded the story saying, "For everyone who sets himself up as somebody will become a nobody, and the man who makes himself nobody will become somebody" (Luke 18:14, MSG).

"Your Honor, she's lying. The accident didn't happen like she says. She was the one who cut in front of me and caused the crash," said the one.

"Not at all, Your Honor. She's the liar. I was parked, when she went by really fast; she lost control in the curve and crashed into my parked car," said the other.

The first one came back. "Those are more lies, Your Honor, because after the crash, her car ended up in the middle of the street, which means she wasn't parked, but she pulled out without looking, the sun blinded her, then she cut in front of me and crashed into my car."

But the second came back again. "Your Honor, it's that *she is also lying* because she says that the sun got in my eyes. How could the sun blind my eyes if it was at my back?"

But then the judge took a turn. "Wait a minute," he roared, addressing the last speaker. "Lady, tell me, if *she is also lying*, and you two are the only ones talking, then *who else is lying*? Your own words have given you away. You are the other one who *is also lying!* Pay the

$8,000 dollars in damages and court costs, and be grateful I'm not locking you up for perjury!

The one who cannot lie said, "by your words you will be justified, and by your words you will be condemned" (Matthew 12:37, NKJV). Proven true by the two women of our story. But on a certain occasion, Jesus was in the temple when two men came in. One, a puffed up Pharisee, prayed with himself saying, "God, I thank you that I am not like other people, robbers, evildoers, adulterers, or even like this tax collector. I fast twice a week. I give a tenth of all my income." He was lying because, indeed, he was like others. He was pompous and boastful, stepping on the publican's mud, so he wouldn't get his own feet dirty. But the publican, who lived from lies and deceit (overcharging for the taxes he collected), told the truth: "However the tax collector stood at a distance and would not even lift his eyes up to heaven, but was beating his chest and saying, 'God, be merciful to me, a sinner!" (Luke 18:13, EHV). Jesus concluded the story saying, "For everyone who sets himself up as somebody will become a nobody, and the man who makes himself nobody will become somebody" (Luke 18:14, MSG).

Somewhere else in Scripture we are warned not to make God a liar, that is to give false witness about God (1 John 1:10). We make God a liar when we say that God forgives us for our penance, or for the great sacrifices we make, or for how much pain we take for him, or for the evil we quit doing, or for whatever changes are taking place in our lives. Jesus said it spot on: "Let your statement be, 'Yes, yes,' or 'No, no.' Whatever goes beyond these is from the Evil One" (Matthew 5:37, WEB). To say, "Yes, yes" is to point to the cross and exclaim, "Yes! There is the Lamb of God in my place taking away my sin!" To say, "No, no" is to say, "No, his sacrifice was not enough; he needs my pious efforts in transforming my life; he needs me to show him how much I love him; he needs me to suffer, to do the best I can." It is then that we make God a liar, for on the cross he exclaimed, "It is finished!" I have done everything you need to be made right before God. And then he opens the windows of heaven and pours out faith to overwhelm us, and as that downpour engulfs us, we worship saying, "Yes, yes, your will be done!"

8
Hair Doesn't Lie

> "She stood behind him at his feet weeping, [and] she began to wet his feet with her tears. Then she wiped them with her hair, kissed them and poured perfume on them . . . Then Jesus said to her, 'Your sins are forgiven" (Luke 7:38, 48, NIV).

A certain day a woman came to Family Law requesting sole custody of her children. Previously, the judge had given sole custody to the father. She now alleged that the father inflicted mental cruelty on the children, screaming threats of physical abuse to them and the mother. She now had to intervene to protect her children. The Child Protection Agency, at the father's request, had already investigated the case. The report read that the mother lived in a dirty, cockroach-infested garage. The living conditions posed a danger to the children. Months back, the mother had been sentenced for personal use of cocaine, and she was still on probation. That's why the investigators had permission to search the premises, and as part of the evidence, they took several strands of the mother's hair to examine them for drug toxicity. They apply certain chemicals to the hair, and the test detects the presence of any drug use during the past three months. They had also investigated the father, taking some of his hair as well. The children reported they were happy living with the father, but did not enjoy the mother's visits. Even so, the judge was not convinced. He wanted the mother to have at least partial custody. As the attorneys were articulating their case, the court clerk interjected. She told the judge the drug test reports were already in the file before him. As he read them, a large frown appeared on his forehead. "Madam," he said addressing the mother, "did you know you have a recent dirty drug test?"

Now it was the woman's turn to scowl. "That's impossible, Your Honor. I haven't used in almost a year, or had a test in months!"

"Well, madam, that's right. Your blood hasn't been drawn for a blood test, but we tested strands from your hair, and hair doesn't lie! The mother's petition for sole custody is denied! Moreover, the district attorney's office will file new charges for drug use during probation. So ordered!"

Scripture teaches us that all the strands of our hair are counted (Matthew 10:30). But what if a hair test could be done to see all our thoughts of anger, vengeance, and lust, among other vices, during the past three months? Let us suppose that each hair contains a microchip in which all our intentions, doubts, resentments, and envy would be recorded, and then downloaded to a text file . . . How large would be the file? How many pages? Would you want them posted on Facebook? What would be the result of that test: clean or dirty? The heavenly court only wants to see clean tests on its file. But what if a moral test could be done on a strand of Jesus's hair? What would that result look like? It would show an entire life – from birth to the cross – of the purest and most self-giving love. Full of his mercies even when we doubt in him, or blame him for all the bad things that happen to us, or when we take his name in vain and blaspheme his name with our mouth or our actions. He did pass the hair test. His love and grace are so great toward us that when we approach the heavenly court, Jesus steps in and shows his clean test report as if it were our own. He says, "My purity is your purity, my love is your love." Our own record never appears before the judge. He only looks at the file of his Son and is well pleased. But what happens to our file? "He will again have compassion on us; he will tread our iniquities underfoot. You will cast all our sins into the depths of the sea" (Micah 7:19, ESV). That is why Mary washed Jesus's feet with a perfume of great price, and dried them with her hair. "And Jesus said to her, "Your sins are forgiven." (Luke 7:48, NIV). That was forgiven hair. Hair doesn't lie!

9

She Cursed Me With The Crucifix!

> "After disarming the rulers and authorities, [God] made a public display of them by triumphing over them in Christ" (Colossians 2:15, EHV).

"So, at what moment do you remember waking up?" asked the district attorney.

"Well," answered the middle-aged woman at the witness stand, "I woke up when she landed the first blow with the crucifix, and opened up my lip."

"And, where was she?" continued the attorney.

"Well, as she hit me, she was also landing on top of me. Once there, she kept hitting me with the crucifix. I covered my face with my hands and arms. Then I rolled to my side to slide off the bed, but that's when she opened up my scalp with the crucifix."

"Was the defendant saying something to you as she hit you?"

"Yes, she was cursing me really bad. She was saying that I had cast a spell on her husband with that crucifix, and that's why he left her for me, so she was returning a thousand curses and bad spells with the same crucifix. That the spell she was casting on me was for me to get eaten up by worms in hell."

"And what happened next? At what point did she stop hitting you?"

"Well, I slid off the bed the best I could, then crawled out the door while she kicked and hit me. I could only scream. When I finally got up, my neighbors were there to help me. She took off running, but my neighbors got a hold of her and didn't let her go. Finally, she threw the crucifix at me still pronouncing curses and spells."

"Madam," asked the attorney, "do you believe in curses and spells?"

"No sir, I don't believe in that stuff. Whatever evil we have, we carry it inside us. But that crucifix is a curse when it's used like a weapon; she almost killed me."

In the time of Christ, to hang on a cross meant you were accursed by God. In other words, even God had rejected and abandoned the one crucified. It was based on the Scripture: "for anyone hung on a tree is under God's curse" (Deuteronomy 21:23, CSB). Legally, that was the only reason why God allowed the death on the cross of his Son, because the law said that anyone who hung on a tree was accursed and condemned by God. The Romans sentenced him to the cross, and Jesus did not elude the sentence. He was hung on that tree. And when the law found him, it cursed and condemned him as a delinquent hanging on a tree.

But Jesus did not suffer the cross just to fulfill the law's requirement. That was not his purpose in giving himself over to the tormentors who hung him to that tree. He went to the cross to take the curse that you and me, and the entire human race deserves. He was cursed in our place with the curse we deserve. "It was certainly our sicknesses that he carried, and our sufferings that he bore . . . He was pierced because of our rebellion and crushed because of our crimes. He bore the punishment that made us whole; by his wounds we are healed" (Isaiah 53:4-5, CEB).

The cross served as a lightning bolt to catch every curse against us; that is why we are no longer cursed, nor can any curse come against us. Every curse directed at us is deflected to the past and falls on his body, pure and holy. To him who believes, no human or devilish spiritual curse or action can bring any harm. The cross is the place where God's power strips all Satanic curse from its power. It was there that God, having disarmed "the rulers and authorities, he made a public display of them by triumphing over Christ" (Colossians 2:15, EHV). That is why that very place where Jesus took our curse is at the same time the place where our greatest blessing was poured out. "Christ redeemed us from the curse of the law by becoming a curse for us—for it is written, 'Cursed is everyone who is hanged on a tree'"

(Galatians 3:13, ESV). The curse that the law placed on us was left in his wounds, and that is why from them, we receive the blessing of healing (Isaiah 53:5). Therefore, "you are complete in Him, who is the head of all principality and power" (Colossians 2:10, NKJV).

10

Pregnant and Doing Drugs?

> "I give them eternal life, and they will never perish, and no one will snatch them out of my hand. My Father, who has given them to me, is greater than all, and no one is able to snatch them out of the Father's hand. I and the Father are one" (John 10:28-30, ESV).

It seems cruel. As soon as the girl was born, she was given a blood test. The result was positive for cocaine and methamphetamines. The newborn had all the symptoms of a neonatal addiction. The medical term is "Neonatal Withdrawal Symptoms." It occurs because a pregnant woman takes narcotics such as heroin, codeine, oxycodone, methadone, and others. These drugs penetrate the placenta and are then transmitted through the umbilical cord into the fetus. The fetus also becomes addicted. At birth, the baby is already drug dependent, but since the newborn is no longer receiving the drug, the baby presents withdrawal symptoms. The newborn may exhibit excessive crying or shrieking, irritability, convulsions, profuse sudation or sweating with concomitant dehydration and vomiting. The combination of these symptoms at times is even fatal. In this particular case the Child Protection Department had already suspected such an outcome. They had everything ready. As soon as they had the newborn's positive test results, the baby was immediately taken from the mother's breast and into protective custody. Now weeks later, the mother struggled before the judge for the return of her baby. "It's that I didn't know I was pregnant when I was using!" was her pretext.

"Impossible," the judge exclaimed. "The same thing happened when your first daughter was born! If you'd like to see them, I still have the pictures of her deformities in your file. What I don't have is the picture of the little grave in the cemetery where she was buried! You and the baby's father are charged with providing illicit drugs to a minor and attempted murder of a minor!"

But what about if at the time of our birth, we had been given a sin blood test? What would have been the results? It would show everything that our first parents handed down to us through our spiritual DNA. What if the results were printed? Greed: _______ percent. Selfishness: _______ percent. Lust: _______ percent. Anger: _______ percent . . . and many others. We are born addicted to sin. For the proof, all we have to do is look at a child's development, and we'll see all those evils come along with the product we've brought to life. It hurts us because that child is our own, and we know it's true. But instead of snatching us from his bosom, God placed us in the bosom of his beloved Son. He was sent by God to provide a clean blood test on our behalf—that is, all of us who've been born with "Sin Addiction Withdrawal Symptoms." Then God out of his sovereign mercy decrees that all who believe in that holy infant on Mary's breast is forgiven.

For the sake of Christ, God does not look at our dirty blood test, but on the pure results of the life of his Son, and credits us with his results. Our heavenly father is the Judge in Sinners Court. But he does not turn us over to a foster home until we grow up and turn our lives around. He himself takes us on his own body, and heals us with his stripes. "I give them eternal life, and they will never perish, and no one will snatch them out of my hand. My Father, who has given them to me, is greater than all, and no one is able to snatch them out of the Father's hand. I and the Father are one" (John 10:28-30, ESV). Look, there is your tiny infant hand in God's powerful but loving hands. "Rise, your faith has made you whole."

11

And Why Don't You Meet Halfway?

> "He saved us— not by works of righteousness that we had done, but according to His mercy" (Titus 3:5, HCSB).

"Sir, this man sold me a car that ran for exactly ten minutes. Then, the engine shut off and didn't run again. Nothing in it worked: the water pump, the battery, and a bunch of other things. It's like I threw away $1,200.00!"

We were in the mediator's office. He was attempting for the two parties to come to an agreement. Now, he addressed the seller. "And you, sir, what do you have to say in response to what this lady is saying?"

"Well," he answered, somewhat hesitantly, "it's that I don't even know who this lady is. It's the first time I've ever seen her. How is it possible that I sold her a car when I've never seen her before? Lady, I never sold you any car at all."

"Is that true?" asked the mediator. "Have you ever seen this man before?"

"Well," she also answered with a certain hesitation. "It was Lucho who sold me the car."

Back to the mediator: "Sir, do you know Lucho?"

"Yes, Lucho is one of my associates who works with me. But the cars he sells are his, not mine," answered the presumed seller.

"But this car has your name on the sales receipt," responded the mediator.

"Well, that's because I own the business, but I don't own all the cars I sell."

"You see?" interjected the woman. "They've got a scam going on. That's how they take advantage of people; they make all that up and sell worthless cars."

"Alright, sir. What do you offer the lady to resolve this case so that neither of you has to come before the judge? If you can't agree, the judge will decide. One will win, the other will lose," proposed the mediator.

"Well," said the man. "she can have $600, and I'll give her $300 cash today."

"No!" retorted the woman. "I can't accept that miserly offer. I want my $1,200 back!"

"But think about it, madam. Can't you meet each other halfway?" proposed the mediator once again.

Before the Superior court above, there's no such thing as meeting God halfway. That is, that God takes care of half of what I owe, because of Christ's life. But I pay for the other half with my efforts, good works, loving obedience, and good character. We cannot meet God's righteousness at the halfway point. Scripture assures us that "all our righteous deeds are like a filthy cloth" (Isaiah 64:6, NRSV). Thus, they are worthless, and God rejects them with abhorrence. They offend his perfect righteousness. How could it ever occur to us to offer him filthy rags to repay our debt? We owe God not only our life, but the debt for all our hypocrisy, lack of sincerity in our love, pretending to be something we're not, hatred of our neighbor, and despising God's grace and mercy. Because our works, even the best and most cherished ones, arise from a sinful being, they don't even amount to a penny. In fact, they place us in greater debt. Not even our good intentions are any good, or even our best and purest thoughts. On the other hand, a life of sin and a history of breaking his law of love for neighbor and self sum up to the same zero total. It's the same with an out of control, pleasure-seeking life which justifies itself saying it's only being honest with one's self.

But there is one who paid for all, and every single moral debt we have accumulated. With his death, he paid for our death, so that we may live again in him. The debt is cancelled. The life of love at its fullness and the purest affection required of us, he lived on our behalf.

He's done this even for the most undeserving sinner. "He saved us—not by works of righteousness that we had done, but according to His mercy" (Titus 3:5, HCSB). He is the one "who pardons all your guilt, who heals all your diseases . . . He does not treat us as our sins deserve. He does not repay us according to our guilty deeds" (Psalm 103:3, 10, EHV). What room is there then, for meeting him halfway, when the Mediator himself has met us the entire way?

12

Dead Fly or Double Faced?

In these last days, God has spoken to us by his Son" (Hebrews 1:2, NIV). "Her sins, which are many, have been forgiven" (Luke 7:47, NASB).

Two women, barely in their twenties, appeared before the Family Law judge requesting a Stay-away order from the other. It was a complicated situation. One of them was the ex-girlfriend of the other's boyfriend. But before they had split up, she'd had a baby with him. That little girl was now in daycare. The two parents, although no longer a couple, shared custody. That meant that the girl shared court-ordered visitation between mom and dad. The young man's new girlfriend (the other woman in this story) opposed such visitation. She also didn't want her boyfriend (the other's ex) to do any favors for his ex (the little girl's mother). But the toddler's mother had her own request. She didn't want her ex-boyfriend's girlfriend [stay with me] present when the little girl visited her father. "Your Honor, she verbally abuses the baby. She makes fun of her. She tells her she's not as pretty as her own girls."

The two young women shared a history of intrigue and hate. But the new girlfriend claimed to have written evidence to support her Stay-away order petition. It was a page from a social network chat room. The new girlfriend alleged the other woman had sent her a death threat. The words were in Spanish, but the young woman brought her own English translation for the judge. The translation into English seemed incriminating: "You are a dead fly." But although the author claimed responsibility for the note, the Spanish version "*Eres una mosca muerta,*" was not to be taken literally. That it only meant "You are double faced, somewhat like the English phrase "You're a fly on the wall." She claimed that the woman had one face for the people outside her house, but another one for the boyfriend's daughter when she visited her home. But the judge did not accept the metaphoric explanation. He knew enough Spanish to translate "mosca muerta [dead fly]" literally, but not metaphorically. Thus, he ordered the author of the note to stay away from the woman who had received the presumed death threat. Everything was very complicated. The relationship between the man and the two women, the little girl involved caught in the middle, and then the language barrier.

But our heavenly Judge has removed all complications in the human situation with only one name: Jesus Christ. There are no other gods – lovers. He does not share our custody with anyone. He is a jealous God. Neither does he love us one day, abhor us the next, and goes away looking for others more attractive to love. Scripture affirms: "Great is your faithfulness" (Lamentations 3:23, NKJV). He is "The Rock! His work is perfect, For all His ways are just; A God of faithfulness and without injustice, Righteous and just is He" (Deuteronomy 32:4, NASB). This is not just lip faithfulness. Jesus willingly took on the cross, and together with it, all our guilt for every one of our sins. With his sacrifice, he was being faithful to his promise to redeem us and restore us to his side forever! "There is salvation in no one else, for there is no other name under heaven given to people by which we must be saved" (Acts 4:12, CSB). That is the Word of God on the cross. He doesn't need any interpreters, for he was interpreting God's will for you and me faithfully and precisely, without any room for imprecision or ambiguity. On the cross, Christ also demolished all language barriers. Scripture says, "In these last days, God has spoken to us by his Son" (Hebrews 1:2, NIV). And what does that sole interpretation say? In every imaginable language that exists, this is what it says: Though they are many "Your sins are forgiven" (Luke 7:48, NIV). His language is the universal language of forgiveness. He understands even the multiple groans of our hearts when we struggle with our conscience and our uncertainties about the present and the future. We cannot confuse him. He interprets even our sighs longing for unmerited grace, and grants us forgiveness even before the words of repentance are able to form in our lips. In exchange for what? For one atom of faith, which does not even come from us, but is also God's gracious gift of grace to us. For Christ is the Author and the Finisher of our faith (Hebrews 12:2). "This is a true saying, to be completely accepted and believed" (1 Timothy 4:9, GNT).

13

This Is Not Rehab, This Is Slavery!

> "But you are a chosen race, a royal priesthood, a holy nation, a people for his possession, so that you may proclaim the praises of the One who called you out of darkness into His marvelous light" (1 Peter 2:9, HCSB).

The young man was responding to the court for an alleged violation of probation. The police had arrested him at his girlfriend's house, and today was his court appearance. A year ago, he had been stopped at a police checkpoint, and K9 police had found ten pounds of methamphetamines hidden away in his car. The judge had given the young man a break. Instead of putting him in jail, he had sent him to a one-year drug rehab program run by a Christian organization. If for some reason he did not comply, he automatically would get a two-year jail sentence.

I was translating for the twenty-two-year-old as he spoke to his attorney. "Look, man, that's not a rehab program. It's a scam. Instead of classes, they take us from town-to-town begging for donations. I got tired of that, and it seemed unfair. I was there to recover from drugs, not to be used as a beggar. I couldn't even see my girlfriend."

"Well," responded the attorney, "remember that you promised the judge that if you didn't complete the program, he would impose the two-year suspended jail sentence."

"No!" he retorted. "Tell the judge to send me to another program that will really help me."

Minutes later, the lawyer came back. "The judge has a counter offer. Two years in jail. If you behave in jail, you'll only do one.

Otherwise, it's six months in jail, and a year in the same program as before. So what will it be?"

The young man thought for a few moments. "Tell the judge that I'll stay with the same program as before."

"What?" questioned the attorney. "Wasn't that the slavery begging program?"

"Well," was the hesitant answer. "It's that there they also say some very nice things about this guy Jesus."

After, I asked him: "And what do they say about Jesus that you'd rather go back to what you said was slavery?"

"Truth is, I misbehaved, became like a rebel in the program. But I couldn't forget what they were saying about Jesus."

"Like what?" I prompted.

"Well, at first I couldn't believe it. That he had taken my place on a cross, that he had taken my sins and punishment. That he had given his life for me. It was like that story was winning over my heart, but at the same time, I rebelled."

"Rebelled?" I continued.

"Yes. It's that I thought they were throwing a whole bunch of lies at me. I couldn't believe that someone totally innocent would do that for me just out of love. I don't even know what love is, I've felt hatred all my life."

My attention now was fully engaged, so I continued. "And where do they get that story from?" I asked, pretending not to know.

"They get it from a book they call the Word. They're always talking and reading from it. Just from the Word. Frankly, everybody there is like family. They look out for each other, even guys like me that act up and mess things up. And when we go to other towns, it's not just to get donations. We go to the streets where the druggies hang out, and we tell them the same things about Jesus, and we take them to the program."

That was it. I was hearing the Gospel preached from a newly-born brother in Christ. He was also giving the best description of church, the family of the rescued by grace. The Gospel announces that Christ took our place in life and death, and then we retell that story to whoever wants to listen. That's what wins the hearts of rebels and unbelievers. But it must be told and retold, for as a drop of water over the centuries breaks granite, so does the Gospel retold break the hearts of rebels, and those who've never been loved by anyone, not even by themselves.

Yes, we rebel when we hear the Gospel. It sounds too good to be true. We may even act against every one of its principles, but even so, it is winning our heart. The truth of Christ's substitute life is for us, even as we rebel and oppose it. "When you were spiritually dead because of your sins and because you were not free from the power of your sinful self, God made you alive with Christ, and he forgave all our sins" (Colossians 2:13, NCV). "You were once disobedient and rebellious toward God but now have obtained His mercy" (Romans 11:30, AMPC). And this is the result: "But you are a chosen race, a royal priesthood, a holy nation, a people for his possession, so that you may proclaim the praises of the One who called you out of darkness into His marvelous light" (1 Peter 2:9, HCSB).

14

Congratulations Sir, You Are Pregnant!

> "Truthful lips are established forever, but a lying tongue lasts only a moment . . . Lying lips are disgusting to the Lord, but those who act truthfully gain his favor. (Proverbs 12:19, 22, EHV). "Whoever breathes the truth proclaims righteousness" (Proverbs 12:17, EHV).

The mother tearfully insisted before the judge not to grant her ex-husband visitation rights. "He's still using drugs. That's why we separated. He would snort that powder in front of the girls. He'd get all crazy and frighten them. If you let the girls have visits with him, he'll keep on doing the same thing."

"Well," said the judge. "I have the program report. It says he hasn't missed any classes; he participates; he helps others. I have to take into account the evidence in his favor."

"No, Your Honor, he knows how to put on a good show."

"Well," said the judge now to the father, who was listening respectfully. "If I send you right now to get a drug test, what would it be: clean or dirty?"

"Perfectly clean, Your Honor, I'm not using."

"Very well then; go with this order to the lab. All you need is a urine sample; they send the results quite quickly. Come back after lunch."

The man left the courtroom hand in hand with his girlfriend. Three hours later, they were back, and the judge called the man to the stand. After a brief glance at the test, an impish smile crossed the judge's face. "Sir," he addressed the defendant. "Congratulations, you are pregnant!" A muffled, surprised cry came from the audience, as the man's girlfriend quickly rose from her seat and left the courtroom in sobs. "Look young man, you fell in your own trap. You went to the lab with your girlfriend. All our drug tests include a pregnancy test, regardless of the gender. It's automatic. She gave her sample instead of yours. And you see? She didn't even know she was pregnant. Your petition for visits with your girls is denied, and I'm extending your probation for two more years. So ordered!"

Appearances, appearances. We all know how to put on a good show while stuck in our own ruts. Sometimes we lie to cover up our lies, until we're no longer aware what's the truth and what's a lie! Yet, we want it all, regardless of the harm it will bring to others and ourselves, and we'll use deceit to obtain it. Proverbs 12 contains several verses about telling the truth, which we could well direct against the foolish liar of our story – although they also step on our toes. Here are a few, but one of them stands out in this version.[1] If you see it, it's not a typo.

2 A good person will obtain favor from the Lord,
but he will condemn a schemer.
8 A person is praised for the good sense that he speaks,
but a person with a twisted heart will be despised.
13 We trap ourselves by telling lies, but we stay out of trouble by living right.[2]
17 Whoever breathes the truth proclaims righteousness,
but a lying witness is deceitful.
19 Truthful lips are established forever,
but a lying tongue lasts only a moment.
20 Deceit lies in the heart of those who plot evil,
but for those who promote peace there will be joy.
22 Lying lips are disgusting to the Lord,
but those who act truthfully gain his favor.

Did you see it? It's verse 17: "Whoever breathes the truth proclaims righteousness."

---

[1] Evangelical Heritage Version.
[2] Contemporary English Version.

Most versions translate the Hebrew word used here as "speaks, utters." But "breathes"? Yet, it is the closest to the meaning of the original. It teaches that truth can be breathed in and out. Truth is a spiritual essence that just as oxygen gives life to the blood, so truth is life-giving spiritual oxygen. The opposite, then, is also true. We are able to breathe lies and deceit and oxygenate our spiritual system with nothing but falsehood. Of course, we would like to think we are within the first camp, the truth breathers. But the heart is deceitful and desperately sick, therefore too feeble and frail to even tell the truth (Jeremiah 17:9). One minute we are breathing the pure oxygen of truth, the next we rip off the oxygen mask, desperate for some toxic deceit.

All these texts from Proverbs 12 serve to show that while we may take a few puffs of truth and breathe out a few, we live in a truth deprived environment, and, thus, live toxic lives. But we can go back and forth applying these texts to either what we should be, or using them to reveal what we are not. That is, in fact, the purpose of Proverbs 12, for all these texts belong to the law and serve as a full exposition of the ninth commandment: "You shall not bear false witness (Exodus 20:16, ESV). They cut through the falsehood to the truth of our deceitful heart.

But then what? Are we left only with a sense of shame and dissatisfaction with ourselves, with a gnawing sense of condemnation for not doing better?

Jesus said that "the Law of Moses, the Prophets, and the Psalms" testify of him, particularly of his sacrifice (Luke 24:44, NIV). In the Hebrew Bible, the Proverbs belong to a section of the Psalms. Thus, we may safely conclude that the Proverbs 12 texts about deceit and the truth are designed to lead us away from ourselves (the residence of deceit) to him who is the truth.

When he said, "I am the way, the truth, and the life" he was stating precisely that he is the one who is able to breathe truth, and nothing but the truth. The truth is the essence, the oxygen of who he is, what he breathed in at his first breath in that manger in Bethlehem. And when he breathed his last, it was his life-giving breath to humanity. That is why the tomb could not contain him, because the truth is the breath of life, and the truth cannot die.

That truth, which he spoke at every step of the way, from birth to his ascension was this: "Because of my perfect life on your behalf, and my death in your place, your sins have been forgiven forever." That is the truth. Breathe it in; breathe it out. It's pure oxygen for eternal life.

15

Put Up A Smokescreen, That's It

> "For the Lord does not look at things the way man does. For man looks at the outward appearance, but the Lord looks at the heart" (1 Samuel 16:7, EHV).

There are some drug offenses that can disappear with a rehabilitation program. One of them is called PC1000. It's for first time offenders. Judgment is deferred for eighteen months, allowing offenders to complete a program of counseling and group therapy. They have to attend at least one class/group therapy session per week for sixteen weeks, pay a small amount for each meeting, submit to random drug testing, and avoid any other criminal activity. If they finish the program successfully, their guilty plea is lifted, and their record is sealed; it's as if they had never committed the offense. On a certain occasion, a handsome young man showed up with his class to receive his certificate of completion. I remembered him from the beginning of the program. He had promised he would complete the program as mandated. Obviously, he had done it to the letter of the law. The judge gave a speech of congratulations and personally stepped off the bench to congratulate him with his group of successful program graduates.

Afterwards, in the hallway, I also congratulated him. But he pulled me aside and whispered: "Look, it wasn't all that bad. Yes, I did learn some good things; I won't deny it. But I hated going to the classes; I had to pay for all the meetings. I stuck with it because otherwise I would have gotten kicked out of my job for doing drugs. But you know what? If you're smart, you learn how to put up a smokescreen and do whatever you want; they don't even notice." He added a wink for emphasis with a mischievous smile, then added: "But at the end, you get a certificate, see? Ha, ha ha! Yes, I complied."

Such is the keeping of the law. In this world, before your social media, the church, employers, friends, you get may get a certificate, but before God? Who laughs then? "But the Lord laughs at the wicked, for he knows their day is coming" (Psalm 37:13). All law keeping, with the intent to win God's favor, is nothing but wickedness, and God laughs at its worthless value, at all the efforts to comply. "For no one will be justified in his sight by the works of the law, because the knowledge of sin comes through the law" (Romans 3:20, HCSB). After all your efforts at keeping the law with an eye at obtaining a "saved certificate," all you get is another certificate. It's the Certificate of Condemnation. It says, "You've got a sinful heart, and your efforts at law keeping didn't get rid of it, you have failed. Thus, you are condemned!"

So, what do you do? Try and try again? Or do you hope that your law-keeping works as a smokescreen before God, and your heart incompliance goes unnoticed? That somehow you will outsmart God at his salvation game, or that you will emerge out of the divine courtroom with an "eternal salvation" voucher?

Remember the rich young ruler? He came to Jesus for confirmation that he already had earned his pass. He thought perhaps Jesus – as a Good Teacher – could give him the voucher, or look him up in the heavenly computer and confirm he was already in the database of the saved.

So, he gave all the right answers when questioned about his participation in the program. "You know the commandments: 'You shall not commit adultery, you shall not murder, you shall not steal, you shall not give false testimony, honor your father and mother'" (Luke 18:20, NIV).

To which he quickly answered: "I have obeyed all these commandments since I was a young man."

But the Judge came back: "You lack one thing." One thing so important that he was *not* going to get his coveted certificate of "heir of eternal life."

Over the years, much has been said about the identity of this "one thing." In fact, it seems it was more than one. It was four: sell, give, come, and follow. "Sell all you have and give it to the poor, and you will have treasure in heaven. Then come, follow me." So, did the young man lack more works? Did he now need to keep four more commandments?

No. Those additional four things were intended to rid him of everything he had brought to Christ. If he had complied, what would he have left?

Nothing.

Except Christ alone. He would have come back empty, but only to be filled with the fullness of Christ. He would have come back naked, but only to be dressed with Christ's robe of righteousness. The treasure of heaven—His righteousness, his obedience, and his love. He would have everything needed, and to overflowing. He would have been richer than before, but only with Christ's eternal and infinite inheritance. Anything else we bring is nothing but a smokescreen. And every time we bring something of our own, we'll only be sent back to get rid of it until we come back with Christ alone. It is only Christ, and Christ alone. He is our only treasure for this life, and for the life to come.

16

Life Or Death Sentence?

> "Carrying his own cross, he went out to what is called the Place of a Skull . . . There they crucified him" (John 19:17-18, HCSB). "Father, forgive them, for they know not what they do" (Luke 23:34, KJV).

You could almost feel the anticipation in the courtroom. At times, there was a tomb-like silence. At others, just a soft murmur with a nervous giggle or two. But we all knew why we were there. In a few moments, the jury would enter and give its sentence on a murder case. The defendant had already been found guilty. The jury had been deliberating on only two choices for the punishment: Life in the state penitentiary, or the death sentence. Due to the seriousness of the case, the law would not grant any other choice. The defendant was still a young man. But the crime had been committed ten years before when he was only nineteen. The matter had taken ten years to reach the sentencing phase. He came from a well-to-do family, where education was highly valued. But the young man had chosen instead to join a criminal gang. The drug lords, for it was also a drug trafficking enterprise, had decreed a death sentence on a high-ranking member of a rival gang. They had chosen two members to deal the fatal blow. They had their orders: the rival must die at their hands. On the appointed day, they stalked the victim, and, as planned, the older boy shot first, causing only minor wounds. The younger man – the defendant in our story – fired the second shot at point blank. Ten years later, it was he awaiting his sentence. His buddy in crime had already been sentenced to life in prison. Now it was his turn. The twelve jurors walked in, somber faced. They had been deliberating for several days, but now they had their verdict ready. The spokesperson handed it to the judge, who gave it to the court clerk for the official reading. "The unanimous sentence of this jury is the DEATH PENALTY . . ."

"Damn you all!" shouted the defendant several times at the jurors. "You are all full of. . . .!" Shaking with fury, he bowed his head on the table while pounding it with his arms and fists, shouting multiple obscenities in a ceaseless fit of fury. He had to be escorted out of the courtroom by the bailiffs. His profanities were still heard from afar, even after the doors were closed.

The scene changes to another courtroom some two thousand years ago. There is the accused, wearing a shameful crown of thorns on his head, also awaiting his verdict. The frenzied crowd shouts it riotously: "Crucify him, crucify him, send him to death!" But this defendant does not bow his head in anger but in prayer. With a whispered plea, he confirms his mission, "Father, forgive them, for they know not what they do" (Luke 23:34, KJV). They were handing out the death sentence to the only one who could give them life. Even as they shouted their obscenity-laced anger at him, he was bearing in his own being all that fury, hate, and everything else behind it. He was also bearing our sinful life, although none of us deserved it. He took on our own broken being on him. No part of us was left out. He embraced all our envy, lust, greed, selfishness, and all our sinful shortcomings, all of who we are. His physical distress was muted by his spiritual anguish, as he became sin for us in Gethsemane, Pilate's courtyard, and then on Calvary. But when he rose from the dead, he left it all inside that tomb. He emerged free from our sins to announce to us that by faith today, he has freed us from our sins!

Yet we insist – through our lack of faith in what he did for us – to still carry them, with their condemnation and oppression. Through our unbelief, we still curse, blame, and blaspheme him even with every breath of air we inhale – and exhale. Who then, is death guilty? But although he could see – through his love that pierced the barriers of time and space – that we would not believe him, he did not step back, back down, or come down from the cross. "Carrying his own cross, he went out to what is called the Place of a Skull . . . There they crucified him" (John 19:17-18, EHV). "He was oppressed, and he was afflicted, yet he did not open his mouth. Like a lamb he was led to the slaughter, and like a sheep that is silent in front of its shearers, he did not open his mouth" (Isaiah 53:7, EHV). And when he gave up his spirit, it was you who died. And when he took his first breath at his resurrection, it was you who breathed it—that was your new birth into eternal life. His doing, dying, and rising again were all in our place, because there's no way we can come before God's presence and live in our condition as sinners.

In exchange for what? The purity of your love for him? The success of your transformed life? Your victories over sin? The fulfillment of your holy life? Your growth in sanctification? Your innocent living before your neighbor?

In exchange for nothing. Because everything we bring is saturated with our sins and sinfulness. Even that young man's fury in the courtroom, his obscenities, his anger, all of which is also latent within us, was borne in Christ's body. Together with all who were watching—judge, jurors, clerks, bailiffs, and us readers here today—we were all in his heart as he redeemed us in the purity of his own soul. There was not a single aspect of our lives that he did not redeem—and for all humanity. "By His stripes we are healed" (Isaiah 53:5, NKJV). That is why he exclaimed in the pain it caused – and the joy of "mission accomplished": "It is finished" (John 19:30, NIV). Your salvation is an accomplished fact. And so is your new sentence: "LIFE AND LIFE EVERLASTING!" in Christ Jesus our Lord. So yes, we can shout with blessings, pour out blessings, dance with joy, and in that craziness of delight we will be escorted into God's presence and enter into his joy forever!

17

Instead Of Punishment, I'll Give Her Another Chance

> "Come now, let's settle this," says the LORD. "Though your sins are like scarlet, I will make them as white as snow. Though they are red like crimson, I will make them as white as wool" (Isaiah 1:18, NLT).

"Magaly Silva [fictitious name], please report to Juvenile Hall, courtroom two." The announcement repeated several times on the courthouse public address system. Finally, a well-built man entered the room. His short sleeve shirt showed well formed biceps and a muscled chest formed by years of hard work in the agricultural fields.

"Well, obviously you are not Magaly Silva," joked the judge, displaying good humor.

But the man was all business. "No, Your Honor, Magaly is sixteen, and she's quite thin."

"Well then, what is your relationship to Magaly?"

"She's my daughter, Your Honor."

"Mr. Silva, it's also quite obvious that Magaly isn't here. Where is she?"

"I don't know, Your Honor. Before I left for work this morning, I told her she had an appointment here at the courthouse this afternoon. I've called her many times, but she doesn't answer her cell phone. I think she's scared."

"Scared?" questioned the judge. "Scared of what?"

"Her grades, Your Honor. You probably have them in the file. She doesn't go to school; she won't do her homework."

"That's true, sir. She is also truant from school; that's why the school issued this summons for her," added the judge.

"I'm sorry, Your Honor. I try to be a good father to her."

"It's a problem common to that age, sir. But my choice is to give them a chance to improve their grades and attendance instead of locking them up or slapping them with a fine, which they usually don't pay. Tell Magaly to come back in two weeks. Instead of a punishment, she'll find another chance."

Incredible! Two weeks later, Magaly was back. She hadn't missed a day of school and hadn't cut any classes. She had done all her homework and passed all her quizzes and exams. Nothing changes the behavior of a human being like unmerited grace.

No one should fear approaching God. In God's presence, you will find more than another chance. Instead of condemnation, you will find grace. Instead of punishment, you will find forgiveness. Scripture says, "Come now, let's settle this," says the LORD. "Though your sins are like scarlet, I will make them as white as snow. Though they are red like crimson, I will make them as white as wool" (Isaiah 1:18, NLT).

All our evil works – as well as our best good works – are written in the file. However, all of them, good or evil, accuse us of being irresponsible and imperfect—in fact, evil at heart. No wonder we are afraid. But no one has to climb up on any cross to be punished. There's already One who willingly climbed up on a cross, and not for himself, but for us and in our place. Scripture adds, "God was reconciling the world to himself in Christ, not counting people's sins against them" (2 Corinthians 5:19, NIV). In the story of our truant girl, the judge was willing to give her another chance on the condition of improving her grades. But in the story of Calvary, it is Christ himself who shows his perfect grades as if they were ours. And all his grades are above excellent; there is no fault anywhere at all. This is grace, love, and forgiveness. The slate is wiped clean. Your faults are totally erased by the blood of Christ. And we start with a clean slate. But the slate will never again be tarnished. Because it will be filled with the works of Christ, and his grades will never change. Yes, Christ's grades will be placed in your file, and, thus, you will never be given a failing grade. But do you need changes in your life? Nothing changes the human being like unmerited grace!

18

I Should Have Thought Before Taking The Wheel

> "For the Law was given by Moses, but grace and truth came by Jesus Christ" (John 1:17, KJV).

"Look, counselor," he said to his attorney in the interview room. "You don't understand me. I simply can't go to jail."

"I'm afraid it's you who does not understand me," replied the lawyer. "After your last DUI, the judge warned you that he was hanging 120 days jail time over your head if you were caught driving drunk for the third time."

"But, can't you see my wife is seven months pregnant? If the judge locks me up, my wife is going to be left out in the street! You all want to see her out on the streets with our three children? She doesn't work. I'm the sole provider for my family. What is she going to do? Deliver her baby out in the street?"

"Believe me," responded the attorney. "I understand you. I'm on your side. The problem is the district attorney. They represent the law, and the law has no feelings; it doesn't understand anything. The law doesn't have the least bit of sympathy for your wife's pregnancy, or the risk your family runs of ending up in the street."

"I know," said the young man, somewhat thoughtfully, "but talk to them again. I can't pay with jail time. I'll pay with money, fines, work, classes, but not with jail, I can't."

"Ricardo, we've already talked about this. Do you remember what the district attorney told me the last time I spoke to her about your wife's problem, and that your family could end up in the street?"

At that moment the defendant focused his attention on a buzzing fly at the far end of the room. "I guess I should have thought about all that before I sat behind the wheel. Now I don't know what I'm going to do." Too late for that. But neither does the law understand about regrets.

The law is written with unfeeling letters, whether in stone, papyri, wood, or paper. It doesn't feel the least bit of sympathy, happiness, pity, or any other emotion whether you obey it or not. The law does not congratulate you when you keep it. It doesn't cry when you break it. It only knows how to accuse you and execute judgment when you step on it.

And now we are talking about God's holy law. This law is so demanding that it requires constant compliance. It does not allow for even one slip from anyone – in thought or in deed – no matter who they are. It is so demanding that when it reviews all human behavior, it issues this sentence: "There is no one righteous, not even one" (Romans 3:10, NIV). No matter how righteous, good, and loving a person may appear to be, God's law will always declare him: disobedient, sinful, self-righteous, an assassin, perverse, wrathful, and deserving of the death penalty. But why? Because the law's standard is like the bar at the high jump event. It is always set higher than you can jump, yet it is there for you to try. If you make the new height, then the bar is set higher, even though it's impossible for you. We could always be purer, more patient, and more loving with cleaner hearts, hands, mouth, feet, and eyes than what we have achieved today. When you think you've jumped over it, the bar is then set even higher. How much higher can you jump? How many more jumps do you have left in you?

But when God's law measures Christ's life, that's when the law starts to feel. It feels ashamed, humiliated, outdone, and overpowered; it wants to hide. Why? Because the life of Christ surpassed all of the law's demands. Christ's moral perfection is infinite. The law's moral code is unable to describe the infinite reaches of who he has been, who he is, and who he shall be, and all of who he is. The apostle John explains it like this: "For the Law was given by Moses, but grace and truth came by Jesus Christ" (John 1:17, KJV). This particular combination of "grace and truth" is lacking in the law of Moses, which is in the Ten Commandments, and all other laws that derive from it. In the Ten, there was (and is) only "condemnation and truth." But "grace and truth" describe who Jesus is, and what he did for us. His work of grace for us is divine truth for us, and that truth is eternal and unfailing.

His truth of the forgiveness of our sins has our name written on it. It is given to us by grace alone; it is not of works. We cannot take any credit for who he is. It seems so ridiculously obvious to state it, but our human heart is always looking for a way to get credit for even a tiny bit of the action, so that it has to be stated: We cannot take any credit for what he has done for us, and who he is for us. God's work in Christ was entirely out of our volition. It was entirely God's initiative and doing from beginning to end, to love and redeem you. And it was freely given to us, entirely out of his mercy for us. It didn't cost us anything, not even faith. For saving faith is also God's initiative in Christ, who is the Author and Finisher of our faith. But our salvation did cost Jesus everything, including descending into the unknown realms of the "valley of the shadow of death" on our behalf. We don't know, neither do we have the slightest idea of the grief he experienced in his being. But as he entered that darkness, he was becoming sin for us, and in taking on the sin of all humanity, became the greatest sinner ever before the sight of God. No wonder he exclaimed, "My God, my God, why have you abandoned me!" The divine God, becoming us in our judgment, felt abandoned by the divine God, as he entered our darkness. But when he, who is the light, shone in that darkness, the darkness could not overcome his mercy! Think about it: our darkness could not overcome his grace. To God alone be the glory!

19

Playing With Fire

> "By faith Abel offered a better sacrifice to God than Cain did. By faith he was commended in Scripture as righteous; God testified favorably about his gifts. And by faith he still speaks, even though he is dead" (Hebrews 11:4, MSB).

Two brothers appeared before the judge. One was fifteen, the other sixteen. The presumed crime? Possession of a lighter on school grounds. The security guard found them playing with fire and gave them a summons to appear before the judge. Now each one was appearing separately. The youngest one was up first. "Tell me, young man, why did you have a lighter in your pocket?"

He responded, "It's that at home we have to light the burners for breakfast, and I carelessly left it in my pocket."

"But isn't there any other way to light the burners?" replied the judge.

"No, Your Honor. It's an old gas stove. You have to turn the lever to let the gas escape, then you light it up with the lighter," answered the boy.

"Let's say for a moment you're right, young man. But, could it also be that just by chance, you use the lighter to light up a joint?"

"No, Your Honor!" he replied a little too forcefully. "I would never touch that weed."

"Alright, young man, let me think about it for a few minutes. Let's call the next case."

The young man left, and in walked his older brother. The questions and the answers were the same. Until the judge asked about the joint.

"Yes, Your Honor. I do use the lighter to light up the joint; I confess it."

The judge immediately came back: "And do you also know anyone else who smokes as well?"

"Well, Your Honor, I don't know if my brother told you, but he also . . ."

"That's enough," interrupted the judge. "Don't say anymore." The last one was forgiven, but the first was sentenced. Three months picking up trash from the roads Saturdays and Sundays, from 7:00 a.m. to 5:00 p.m.

At the beginning of the Scriptures, we find that God summoned two brothers to appear, Cain and Abel. "You have sinned against each other, and thus you have sinned against me. Bring the sacrifice that I taught your parents." Days later, Cain appeared. He was bringing an enormous platter full of the most beautiful ripe fruits and vegetables. He had cultivated them with great effort and was proud of his work. It seemed as if he said, "Oh God, there's nothing for which I need to be forgiven. Look at this small harvest: It's perfection! I love my little brother, but compare what we bring. He's careless and doesn't work as hard as I do. As for me, here's the evidence of my work and wisdom in agriculture in this beautiful platter."

A while later, Abel came before God with a little lamb. "This is the sacrifice you taught our parents. It is the promise of a human Lamb who will come and be sacrificed for our sins, and I confess that I have sinned. I don't deserve the forgiveness that you promise in this lamb, but I offer it to you trusting in your grace and mercy."

"And the Lord looked favorably on Abel and his offering, but he did not look favorably on Cain and his offering" (Genesis 4:4-5, ISV).

Cain's reaction shows what was truly in his heart: pride and hate. He was so angry that his offering had been rejected that he rose up and killed his brother out in the field. And yet, he boasted of his good fruits and the perfection of his works. "By faith Abel offered a better sacrifice to God than Cain did. By faith he was commended in

Scripture as righteous; God testified favorably about his gifts. And by faith he still speaks, even though he is dead" (Hebrews 11:4, MSB).

And what does your offering say? About whom does it speak? If it talks about you, it's Cain's. If your offering talks and points to Christ's sacrifice, you have been forgiven!

20

All Interest On The Debt Is Forgiven!

> "God made you alive with Christ and forgave all the things you had done wrong. He destroyed the record of the debt we owed, with its requirements that worked against us. He canceled it by nailing it to the cross" (Colossians 2:13-14, CEB).

It was the start of a civil matter proceeding. Immediately, the judge asked if the plaintiff and the respondent had come to some agreement.

"Yes, Your Honor" answered the plaintiff's attorney. "We have this agreement in writing" as he handed the document to the bailiff.

Once in hand, the judge addressed the respondent. "Sir, are you in agreement with this settlement?"

"Well, Your Honor," answered the respondent for himself since he was appearing without an attorney, "I was asked to sign it, but frankly I don't know what that paper says."

"Was the document translated for you from English into Spanish before you signed it?" inquired the judge.

"No, Your Honor, nobody translated it for me" replied the respondent.

"Objection!" interjected the plaintiff's lawyer. "The document was thoroughly explained to him!"

"Not quite!" exclaimed the judge, somewhat on edge. "The objection is mine now. One thing is to explain; another is to translate. I order the court translator to translate the entire document line by line without leaving anything out. Please exit the courtroom and do what I've ordered. Come back when you're done."

When I translated the agreement, line by line, the respondent agreed with each condition until we got to the last one, written in fine print. This one demanded a 10 percent monthly interest on the unpaid debt, adding hundreds of dollars to his obligation. "No, no one told me about this. I don't agree!"

Back in the courtroom, the judge rebuked the plaintiff's attorney for attempting to swindle the respondent. He then canceled any and all interest payments on the debt, thereby forgiving the respondent of hundreds of dollars in monthly payments. Obviously, the judge had read the fine print and ordered the translation. No details escape the judge's knowing eye.

The debtor's great surprise was that the judge forgave all interest on the debt. He didn't have to plead his case before the judge: he was a farm hand, had five children, and had no other source of income. He expected to pay some interest, but not the large percentage the plaintiff wanted. The annulment of interest payments was freely given, unexpected. But of course, he would have been more surprised if the judge had forgiven *the entire debt.* But that is precisely what the divine Judge did with our debt on account of our sins. That debt is payable by death, and nothing less than eternal death. Such is the mystery of God's holiness. Scripture puts it like this: "God made you alive with Christ and forgave all the things you had done wrong. He destroyed the record of the debt we owed, with its requirements that worked against us. He canceled it by nailing it to the cross" (Colossians 2:13-14, CEB). A dead body cannot pay for anything. That's how we were, "dead in sins and trespasses" (Ephesians 2:1, KJV). Dead and with empty pockets. But the debt was canceled, by someone who indeed was alive and could pay. "Nailed to the cross," means on the pure and holy life of Jesus Christ as he hung on that tree.

"Nothing in life is free," is the common wisdom. It is the same with the forgiveness of sins and eternal life. It is not free, nor cheap. It is extremely costly. So much so that only the innocent body of the Son of God could repay it, but at his own cost. We were not billed one single cent, nor was the most insignificant work demanded from us. God's Good News plainly announces to us that fact, and in writing, without any fine print to deceive us. Neither does the Gospel charge us hidden interest—not even the least percentage. Christ paid our entire debt, and we owe *nothing more*. The Judge's all-knowing eye knows the exorbitant amount of our debt, but he also knows we are absolutely unable to pay, and to pay for an unpayable debt.

Ever since our first fetal heartbeat, and even before, we were already in debt. Why? Because we were conceived in Adam's fallen nature, which only means that every newborn is already a sinner. The divine Judge knows it. That is why God conceived the Gospel, the Good News. Christ voluntarily gave himself to repay our debt, even what we ourselves don't even know we owe. That is how the Gospel instructs us. It shows us our ledger of debt, but at the same time it points to the column where it shows that all has been paid, and by whom. Without you having to plead, to explain your case, or present your need. However, that requires faith, for "without faith it is impossible to please God" (Hebrews 11:6, NIV). It's a faith we can't generate. But in hearing the story of how our debt was paid, why, and by whom, saving faith is generated, and we are led to exclaim, "I believe, help my unbelief!"

21

If You Don't Sign, I'll Send You To Jail!

> "When a strong man, fully armed, guards his own house, his possessions are safe. But when someone stronger attacks and overpowers him, he takes away the armor in which the man trusted and divides up his plunder" (Luke 11:21-22, NIV).

I was so furious I could hardly translate the guilty plea declaration. The district attorney, a man at least 6'4", stood tall and, hovering over the small and frail elderly woman, threatened her: "If you don't sign it, I'll send you to jail!"

The woman was losing her home in a low-income area. She lived there with her daughter and two-year-old granddaughter. There was not a man in the house. The daughter worked washing laundry at a hotel to put bread on the table and pay what they could on the mortgage. The elderly woman held the mortgage in her name. She could not keep a job because she suffered from advanced diabetes and was losing her eyesight. But what was her crime? The grass on the front yard had been burnt from the hot sun and lack of water. Where there had been green grass, now dust blew around. The city inspectors had taken note, and charged her with a violation of the municipal code for residential housing.

Even though they had given her an extension to fix the front yard irrigation, she had not been able to comply. The residents could barely get by. Now the grandmother had to sign the guilty plea, pay a $6,0000 USD fine, and fix the problem in sixty days under the threat of jail time. Because she was already behind in her bank payments, she would also lose the mortgage to the house.

She tried signing at the insistence of the district attorney, who kept towering over her. Her failing eyes could not find the line for her signature, and when I placed my index finger over the line, she began to sign on top of my fingernail.

"Hurry up!" cajoled the district attorney. "If you don't sign, I'll tell the judge to lock you up!" Due to lack of funds, the woman was also appearing without a private attorney, and because she didn't know the legal system, she had waived her right to a public defender. She faced the law alone, destitute, and overpowered by the immensity of the legal and banking system, which at that point were already crushing her and her family. It happens. But is this the best human justice offers? Does the strong man always crush the weakest?

On a certain occasion, Jesus told this parable. "When a strong man, fully armed, guards his own house, his possessions are safe. But when someone stronger attacks and overpowers him, he takes away the armor in which the man trusted and divides up his plunder" (Luke 11:21-22, NIV). But what about when the weakest of the weak are attacked and cannot even defend the little dignity they have left? The woman in our story was at the weakest end of human frailty, and had no stronger man, or woman, to defend her. The judge ordered the ruling. The woman left the courtroom, shaking and in tears. A friendly hand guided her out of the courthouse and to the bus stop.

But in our frailty, misconduct, missed deeds, and with all the weight of the law stacked against us, we do have a strong man. Closer than we think—as close as a blink of faith. Sometimes he's not there as we would expect, need, or want him. We would want him riding as Prince Charming to our rescue, with a dramatic flair. But Scripture tells us that because of the strength of his person, the resurrected Christ is always there. We can by faith reach out and receive mercy, forgiveness, and the dignity granted by his personal attention to our need. Scripture describes that strong man in the following story.

> And a woman was there who had been subject to bleeding for twelve years. She had suffered a great deal under the care of many doctors and had spent all she had; yet instead of getting better she grew worse. When she heard about Jesus, she came up behind him in the crowd and touched his cloak, because she thought, "If I just touch his clothes, I will be healed." Immediately her bleeding stopped and she felt in her body that she was freed from her suffering. At once Jesus realized that power had gone out from him. He turned around in the crowd and asked, "Who touched my clothes?" "You see the people crowding against you," his disciples answered, "and yet you can ask, 'Who touched me?' " But Jesus kept looking around to see who had done it. Then the woman, knowing what had happened to her, came and fell at his feet and, trembling with fear, told him the whole truth. He said to her, "Daughter, your faith has healed you. Go in peace and be freed from your suffering." (Mark 5:25-34, NIV).

Perhaps she feared this Christ strong man would also humiliate and strip her of her new-found healing. But as she approaches, Jesus calls her "daughter." The religious authorities had told her that due to her illness she was no longer God's "daughter," but an impure, unclean sinner. But Jesus does the unpredictable. He surprisingly calls her "daughter." And with that simple, endearing term, he justifies her. His word, which cannot lie, reframes her entire relationship to God. She is the Father's beloved daughter. She is so loved that the Father only wants to see her well. Jesus did not ask her to plead guilty for her sins, or confess them, or even take a purification offering to the Temple. He towers above her, yes, but as the stronger man that has tied up and taken away the strong man of her illness. And he frees her from all ties to her illness.

Whatever is binding you for twelve years, or more or less, ask for imaginative faith to approach him as your strong man, and touch the hem of his garment. "The name of the Lord is a strong tower; the righteous man runs into it and is safe" (Proverbs 18:10, ESV). Live free from your accuser and all self-accusations. "Go in peace. You are freed from your suffering." Remember it every single day of your life!

22
The Choice

> And there is a difference between God's gift and the sin of one man. After the one sin, came the judgment of "Guilty"; but after so many sins, comes the undeserved gift of "Not guilty!" (Romans 5:16, GNT).

The attorney spoke to the young mother in the interview room while a precious three-year-old boy opened the drawers to his desk. "The social worker's recommendation is that you have shared custody. The father successfully completed his anger management, child abuse, and drug rehabilitation program. The law contemplates that each child grows up nourished by a good relationship with both parents. You may accept the recommendation or request a trial before the judge to contest the shared custody with the father. What is your decision?"

Meanwhile, the boy had found a candy in one of the drawers, and with huge wide-open eyes, he fell on his mother's lap as if he understood the conversation. "It's that I don't know what to do. You know this man. You have his record. He's been very violent with the boy. He gave him a terrible beating once and has belted him several times since. Don't you remember the pictures? Will you guarantee me that after a visit with his father, he's not going to come back in a casket? What do I do? What do I do? What is your recommendation?" was her desperate plea.

The attorney, who also happened to be a woman, replied thoughtfully. "I cannot recommend anything to you. I am here to be your advocate before the court for whatever decision you make."

The boy would not let go of his mother's skirt or the candy in his hand, as he fixed his eyes on the attorney. "Look lady," she said. It's your decision. I cannot guarantee you anything. Just listen to your mother's heart." And with that, the boy sank his face into his mother's lap.

The mother in our story agonized over her decision. She had to make a choice. She could, and she did. She made a decision for her son. He could not choose. But she could. She contested the recommendation for shared custody. And she won. The father never again requested either custody or visitation. No one will ever know if that decision was best for the boy. But the mother made that decision for him. The three-year-old could not make it for himself.

It is not all that different for us. Long ago, two contenders disputed our eternal custody. The choice was made when our father Adam gave away our custody. And there is a difference between God's gift and the sin of one man. After the one sin, came the judgment of "Guilty"; but after so many sins, comes the undeserved gift of "Not guilty!" (Romans 5:16, GNT).

We are born into the custody of a murderer and liar, and the father of lies. To make it worse, our willpower is so corrupted; we cannot choose to bail out. We are like that three-year-old. Even our willpower to decide over earthly matters is affected. That's why so many of our choices are self-defeating. So yes, our situation is as bad as it sounds, and worse, because we don't even realize how bad it is. If we are going to get out of our custodian's grip, something big needs to happen, and outside of us.

Indeed, it already happened—in the person of Christ. He was Adam's replacement. Christ, as the new Adam, took on our responsibility to choose on our behalf. In that infant – that newborn in the manger – rode our choice at every instant of his life. That is why he was so bitterly persecuted by the enemy, both to kill him and to seduce him to make wrong choices. But all his life's choices, from birth to Calvary, were made out of disinterested, totally sincere, love for self and others. He fulfilled the greatest of all commandments, "You shall love your neighbor as yourself" (Matthew 22:39, ESV). He took care of himself so he could care for others in every way possible. At each decision-making juncture, he made the most loving and wise choice each time for himself and for others. No one, including the father of our race, has ever made the correct moral and ethical choices at every encounter with good and evil. And no one ever will. Christ's perfect will was enough to cover the insufficient and defective moral willpower of every human being whose heart has ever started to beat upon the face of the earth.

Christ has been the only human being with true freedom of choice. Like Adam, he was free to choose either good or evil. Yet he freely chose the good each time, every time. But from where did he get his motivation and power to freely choose the good consistently? On this regard he said: "My food is to do the will of him who sent me and to accomplish his work" (John 4:34, ESV). His will was nourished by knowing that he was actually doing the will of the Father and accomplishing the task he'd been given. And what was that? To perfectly will the love of God at each instant of his life, and *for us.* We live, because he chose life for us. He willed grace for us, which was the will of the Father for him. And his choice is ours by faith alone. All the fullness of his perfect freedom of choice, God counts as our very own.

But doesn't Scripture say, "Choose you this day whom ye will serve"? (Joshua 24:15, KJV). Yes. And Jesus heard and answered that call of the prophet on our behalf. At every instant, in all places, and throughout all circumstances, he chose to serve the will of the Father.

But what about our moral and ethical choices now? Oh yes. We have them, and we better – for our sake and for the benefit of others – make the very best moral and ethical choices we can make. But these will not alter the choice for our salvation.

That choice has already been made for us.

23

This Child Will Be Your Salvation

'I came that they may have life and have it abundantly" (John 10:10, ESV). "For to us a child is born. To us a son is given. The authority to rule will rest on his shoulders. He will be named: Wonderful Counselor, Mighty God, Everlasting Father, Prince of Peace" (Isaiah 9:6, EHV).

The young woman had just turned eighteen. Her beauty was in full bloom. She had a queen-like demeanor in the courtroom. She was also intelligent, already a sophomore chemistry major at a nearby college. But, and this was her father's "but," she was already six months pregnant. She lived with her dad, who had been a single father to her since her childhood. Since there were only three months left until the arrival of the baby, her boyfriend, and presumed father of the baby, would come over every day to visit her, much to the father's displeasure. In fact, he'd get rather furious.

Today they were all in the courtroom: father, daughter, and boyfriend. The father was requesting a Stay-away order against the boyfriend. But the judge denied all the arguments of the father. The standard for a civil Stay-away order is high. The plaintiff has to demonstrate that there is harassment so continuous and persistent that the alleged victim's life is at grave and imminent danger. But he could only testify that the boyfriend would go to the house, the daughter would let him in, and he and the boyfriend would exchange insults. But then the daughter and the boyfriend would put together furniture and paint the walls in the baby's room.

"That pregnancy ruined my daughter's future. She was well on her way to a career I could never have. I'm a single father; you don't know how much I've sacrificed for her to now lose her to this loser who quit school long ago. Further, I don't have the time or the money to raise a baby at my age. I want him to stay away from our lives forever!"

The judge had listened patiently when finally he interrupted the tirade. "Look, sir. Let me talk to you as a friend, and not as a judge. Pay attention. This child will be your salvation! Make peace with your daughter and this young man. Whether you like it or not, you'll soon be a grandfather. And a grandfather gets older sooner than he thinks. In twenty years, this child will give you his hand when you're tripping over your feet! You've been living alone with your daughter all these years. Well, congratulations! You've got a real family now."

Scripture tells the story of another pregnant young woman. She was engaged to be married. Her boyfriend was very much in love. Slander and gossip flew all around them. Who was the baby's father? Weren't they just engaged? How come she's pregnant? But the young woman had nothing for which to be ashamed, or even less, guilty. When the angel announced to her that she would be a mother by virtue of the Holy Spirit covering her, she responded in faith: "I am the servant girl of the Lord. Let this happen to me as you say!" (Luke 1:38, ICB). And that child growing in her womb did most certainly lend us more than his hand when we were dead in our trespasses and sins after tripping helplessly along into sin. He gave us his life. He was that "holy thing," that new human being for us, at every stage of his life. "And the child grew and became strong, filled with wisdom. And the favor of God was upon him" (Luke 2:40, ESV). Every stage of his human development, from infancy to adulthood, was perfectly lived, and lived to its fullest, on our behalf. Childhood, although a stage of life which surprises us with newly-acquired cognition, loving affection, and abstract thinking, is also a stage in which we begin to see the seeds of selfishness, violence, and greed. From early childhood through late adolescence, we see in children amazing acts of generosity, caring for others, and wisdom. We also see greed, selfishness, bullying, disrespect, and other behaviors that shock their parents and social groups.

Luke reports of an incident where "people were bringing even their babies to Jesus, so that he would touch them" (Luke 18:15, NASB).

Babies? Yes. In fact, the Greek word used here describes both the newly born and the unborn. This is the same word Luke uses to quote the angels' words to the shepherds in the fields, "You will find a baby wrapped in swaddling cloths" (Luke 2:12, ESV). This is a reference to the newborn Jesus in the manger and in Mary's lap. It is also the same word Luke uses to quote Elizabeth when the pregnant Mary comes to visit her: "the baby leaped in my womb for joy" (Luke 1:40, NASB). The word literally means "the unborn" leaped in my womb for joy. It refers to the intrauterine fetus of Jesus. So when Luke reports that "babies" were brought to Jesus to receive his touch, it also includes the unborn. There were pregnant and newly delivered women with their babies that day surrounding Jesus. And with his touch He blessed the born and the unborn. This scene clearly upset the disciples who did not want any woman, particularly those who had just given birth, touching Jesus. The Levitical laws declared them unclean: A woman who becomes pregnant and gives birth to a son will be ceremonially unclean for thirty-three days, and if she delivered a girl, the uncleanness would last for sixty-six days! Thereafter, she had to take an offering before the priest for him to declare her clean (Leviticus 12:1-8). Obviously, the newborn babies were in the arms of "unclean" mothers. To have touched the babies would have meant to have touched the mother as well. But Jesus is the fulfillment of the law, and with his touch he not only restores the mother, but also becomes her offering. But what did the touch mean for the children? "Let the little children come to me, and do not hinder them, for the kingdom of God belongs to such as these" (Luke 18:16, NIV). Through his touch, the newborn and the unborn were born into the kingdom of God!

But what of Jesus himself, when he was a newborn and an infant?

Of him the prophet said, "For to us a child is born. To us a son is given. The authority to rule will rest on his shoulders. He will be named: Wonderful Counselor, Mighty God, Everlasting Father, Prince of Peace" (Isaiah 9:6, EHV).

Indeed, that child became our salvation!

24

My Problem Is That Little Quirk I've Got

> "If you, Lord, kept a record of guilt, O Lord, who could stand? But with you there is pardon, so you are feared" (Psalm 130:3-4, EHV). "As far as east is from west—that's how far God has removed our sins from us" (Psalm 130:12, CSB).

Although the symptoms of her illness were not readily visible, the woman had struggled with thyroid cancer for many years. She told her attorney every possible minutia related to her illness: surgeries, radiation, chemotherapy cocktails, their symptoms and side effects. The medication made her sleepy, her body felt like a ton, she'd lose her appetite, and sometimes become disoriented. Finally, with a certain dramatic flair, she flipped back the hair on her neck, and briefly showed the surrounding surgical scars. One could not help but feel some pity hearing her recount her story, except that it sounded somewhat practiced and dramatized. "Look, I've got here all the proof of my hospitalizations, treatments, and medications I'm taking that leave me dizzy and sleepy half the time. Here are the signatures that I went to Alcoholic Anonymous just like the judge asked me."

The lawyer opened the booklet and noted exactly six signatures, one for each day of attendance. The judge had ordered thirty. "Please allow me," said the young attorney. "I'm going to show all this to the district attorney."

After he left, the lady continued with a touch of anxiety: "Look, you don't know all that I've gone through with this cancer all these years, the surgeries, radiation . . . My only problem is that old little quirk I've got of drinking alcohol. I just had a few little sips before driving to the corner store; it wasn't far. I should have just walked . . ." She kept on talking, but I didn't hear her. I just heard one phrase over again: "My only problem is that old little quirk."

Is that going to be our defense before the throne of God? Is that the best we've got as we face society, our children, our spouse, and our parents? "I'm almost perfect; my only problem is that old little quirk I've got that drives me to do all that I do . . ." Frankly that little word "quirky" fits us all, and to dodge it is also an old little quirk. That "quirk" is nothing less than what the apostle Paul described as a sinful nature, but he used a more descriptive term: the Greek word *sarx* or "flesh." That's our only and old little quirk, our greedy and selfish flesh. It wants to love, but it only wants self-love, and seeks out only its own satisfactions.

The same apostle Paul confessed that with respect to the commandments; he kept all of them, except one: "You shall not covet" (Romans 7:7-11). That was also his old little quirk. His covetousness betrayed him although in his mind he wanted to live free of it and keep the law. But what is the sum of our little quirks? Self-destructive behavior and harm to others.

But God, the Judge of all things, also has an old, huge, infinite quirk: To forgive. Who is a God like you, who forgives guilt, and who passes over the rebellion of the survivors from his inheritance? He does not hold onto his anger forever. He delights in showing mercy (Micah 7:18, EHV). Yes, God always stays centered on forgiveness. "Let us therefore come boldly unto the throne of grace, that we may obtain mercy, and find grace to help in time of need" (Hebrews 4:16, KJV). By giving up his Son to live and die as a sacrifice for our sins, God made an eternal commitment to forgive. That commitment involved this particular "quirk": Jesus Christ would bear our sin and guilt, would be condemned and die in our place, and then freely dress us with all his love, purity, and integrity. In exchange for what? For believing that what God did in Christ is unmovable truth, and that it's all ours through grace by faith alone. That's quite a quirk. God finds the quirkiest sinner along the way and confronts him. Divine quirk versus sinful quirk. "Son, daughter, your sins are forgiven." In Christ, God has taken our sins as far away from us as the east is from the west" (Psalm 103:12). "But with you there is forgiveness so that you may be revered" (Psalm 130:4, CSB). Quirk triumphs over quirk. Always. Take a deep breath. It's true for you—daily and forever!

25

The Law Does Not Penalize You For This Infraction

> "He does not treat us as our sins deserve or repay us according to our offenses. As high as the heavens are above the earth, so great is his kindness toward those who fear him. As far as the east is from the west, so far has he removed our transgressions from us. As a father has compassion for his children, so the Lord has compassion for those who fear him. For he knows how we were formed; he remembers that we are only dust" (Psalm 103:10-14, NCB).

Pale, downcast, and frightened, the woman entered the traffic courtroom. Behind her followed a young adolescent girl with furtive eyes, as if trying to understand her surroundings. They sat in the first row where I would be helping them with the translation of the proceedings. When I briefly greeted them, I realized that the teenage girl had the characteristics of Down syndrome. But before the judge took the bench, the lady tugged at my arm saying, "Tell the judge that the cop gave me this ticket because my girl didn't have her seat belt on. But she has Down's and doesn't know what she's doing. When she gets nervous, she takes it off and then can't put it back on. Tell him we don't have the money to pay the fine." My role in the courtroom is to translate, to merely be a voice between the defendants and the judge, and vice-versa. I cannot advise as an attorney, or plea before the judge on anyone's behalf. The mother was asking me to do something I could not do. I glanced at the girl and suppressed the temptation to intervene on their behalf. At that, the judge took the bench and began roll call. The mother insisted, "Tell him, tell him."

Finally, the judge called their name. He glanced at them and then read a document before him. He then reached over to the volume on Traffic Law, reading over some pages. Finally, the judge addressed them. "Lady, the law does not charge you for this infraction. The matter is dismissed. You may leave the courtroom."

The woman looked at me, wide-eyed. I told her, "Madam, the judge has not charged you for the infraction; you may leave."

"But how much do I have to pay?" she responded. The girl understood faster than her mother. She formed a zero with her thumb and index finger, then changed to a thumbs up and clapped briefly. Then they took each other by the hand and almost danced out of the courtroom.

Such is our condition before God. Scripture says, "He does not treat us as our sins deserve or repay us according to our offenses. As high as the heavens are above the earth, so great is his kindness toward those who fear him. As far as the east is from the west, so far has he removed our transgressions from us. As a father has compassion for his children, so the Lord has compassion for those who fear him. For he knows how we were formed; he remembers that we are only dust" (Psalm 103:10-14, NCB).

The law is blind to our own particular situations. The law only remembers our sins and shortcomings. The law does not remember that, "we are only dust." The law comes down to us as if we were all made of steel, or titanium, or the finest moral materials that could respond and live up to the high pressure of its demands. Thus, even our particular situation condemns us before the law.

But God has another book, another volume before him: The law of grace. When he looks there, he only sees the life of Christ applied to every sinner's particular situation. God does remember that we are but dust and breath, his breath. So, on account of his own breath that he breathed into Adam, made of Eden's dust, he forgives us. Just as we are "God breathed," so we are "God forgiven." How much obedience can dust give, if it is blown away by the first breeze? So, God lets the dust go back to dust. But his breath is the life of Christ on our behalf. And at the resurrection, his glorified breath breathed us up into his life.

Hard to believe? Yes, just like for that mother in the courtroom. But her "Down" daughter was "Up" on the judge's ruling even before she was! Those who need grace the most are the first to get it, to believe that they've been forgiven. "I tell you the truth, unless you turn around and become like little children, you will never enter the kingdom of heaven... Whoever then humbles himself like this little child is the greatest in the kingdom of heaven. And whoever welcomes a child like this in my name welcomes me . . . your Father in heaven is not willing that one of these little ones be lost" (Matt 18:3-5,14, NET).

So, do you get it? Or do you need a Down to give you the thumbs up?

26

She Cared For Him Until He Turned One

> "We love him, because he loved us first" (1 John 4:19, NIV). "See what great love the Father has lavished on us, that we should be called children of God! And that is what we are!" (1 John 3:1, NIV). "I will not leave you as orphans; I will come to you" (John 14:18, NIV).

A sixteen-year-old girl appeared before Juvenile Court in response to a summons initiated by her school. She had missed over fifty percent of school days during the last three months. Her mother was with her. "Magaly, these are way too many absences," chided the judge. "Is there something going on at school that's behind your absences? Not to mention your grades. You are failing all your subjects. Is there someone bullying you?"

"No, sir. I get along with everyone" was her timid response.

"Fine, then" added the judge. "And how are things at home? Are you getting along with your dad, your mom, brothers and sisters?"

"Yes, sir," she answered almost inaudibly. "Everything's ok."

The judge continued: "Is that the young woman's mother back there? Madam, is everything all right back home? What do you think is going on? What's your explanation?"

"Thank you, Your Honor. No, she's behaving at home, gets along well with all of us, her brothers and sisters; everything's fine."

"Well," replied the judge, "help me understand. Why is she not doing well in school?

Something has happened."

"It's that . . ." the mother replied hesitantly. "It's that we used to be a foster home. We took in a newborn boy. Since Magaly was the oldest, she helped me a great deal with his care. Then, after a year, because I was careless and didn't turn in the monthly reports on time, they revoked my license and took the boy away. She had taken care of him from just a few days after birth until he turned one. When they took him away, they ripped her soul away!" A profound silence enveloped the courtroom while the young woman muffled her sobs with her hands . . .

Our first reaction is, of course, to sympathize with the girl. Her maternal instincts had been awakened, and she had bonded with the child. But what about the little boy? He must have bonded with her, and it must have been emotionally traumatic to have been pulled away from her love and affection. It's almost the story of two orphans. Two children left emotionally empty. But the most vulnerable was that little baby boy. What were his chances for recovery . . . to grow up free of the scars? Often, healing comes slowly, but when it occurs, it happens in the least expected scenario.

Scripture tells of a young boy who was also orphaned and disabled in a tragic accident. "Jonathan son of Saul had a son who was lame in both feet. He was five years old when the news about Saul and Jonathan came from Jezreel. His nurse picked him up and fled, but as she hurried to leave, he fell and became disabled. His name was Mephibosheth" (2 Samuel 4:4, NIV). His father and grandfather had been killed in battle. His caregiver, afraid that they would seek the young boy (who was next in line to be king) to take his life, picked him up and ran into hiding. No further details are given about his accident, and how it happened, but he permanently lost the use of both legs. However, that nurse deserved a medal for her courage. A five-year-old boy is no longer an infant, but she carried him, injury and all, and cared for him for many years. She saved his life! But perhaps the young man when able to reason thought to himself: And why did she save me if I was left to deal with life like this? Is this all I can hope for in this life?

The story continues many years later when David remembers his dear friend Jonathan, the boy's father. In his memory, David asks "Is there no one still alive from the house of Saul to whom I can show God's kindness?" (2 Samuel 9:3, NIV). He's told Mephiboshet's story. David immediately sends for him. We can imagine David's men carrying him on a litter for many miles until he reaches the king's palace. The young man is probably trembling in fear. He's been found, and David will finally finish off the house of Saul by taking his life. But he has no idea of how his life is about to change. "Don't be afraid," David said to him, "for I will surely show you kindness for the sake of your father, Jonathan. I will restore to you all the land that belonged to your grandfather, Saul, and you will always eat at my table" (2 Samuel 9:7, NIV). This was the least likely scenario Mephiboshet expected, orphaned early in life, and with a life-long disability. Yet, he is invited to eat forever at the king's table. And as if that wasn't sufficient grace, he is declared the heir of his grandfather's lands.

The surprise ending of that scenario was choreographed by God's grace.

The last thing humanity would have expected from its Creator would have been for God to become human flesh, take its sin and evil on himself, and restore them forever to the King's table. But the cross is God's climactic act of grace to restore and redeem humanity unto himself. The cross is the answer to God's own question: "To whom can I show my kindness?" At the cross, God's kindness was shown to us all, and he invited us all to his table. By faith, let's approach the king's table, and look for our name. We may be afraid, or embarrassed, or curtailed by our physical or spiritual disabilities. But cast all fear and doubt away. By grace, you have been fully restored and made fit to sit at that heavenly table. Look, the king is offering you his cup and a delicious looking piece of bread, the very presence of his eternal life! Take it, eat and drink to its fullest. And rejoice: all the family of history's Mephiboshets surrounds you, and our dad will never leave or forsake us!

27

I Lost Everything To That Man!

> "Therefore God also highly exalted him and gave him the name that is above every name, so that at the name of Jesus every knee will bow, in heaven and on earth and under the earth, and every tongue will confess that Jesus Christ is Lord, to the glory of God the Father" (Philippians 2:9-11, EHV).

She was brought to the courtroom cuffed and shackled. The anger and sadness on her face had a story to tell. But first, the judge arraigned her: "Multiple charges of theft, shoplifting." He then specified the victims, dates, and places. "You are assigned to the public defender."

As the attorney interviewed her, her story came out. "Three years ago, I hooked up with this guy. I thought I was in love, but he fooled me. He said he was a construction worker. Big lie. He was nothing but a thief. Soon after, I got pregnant, and he used me for his business. So, with my big belly, I was nothing but his decoy. He'd take me to the stores, and I'd hide stuff all around my belly. He'd threaten me that if I didn't help him, he'd report me to immigration. We lived off stolen stuff. Everything I was able to pull from the stores, he'd sell at the flea markets and the pawn shops. We already had an established route. One of those days, I went into the corner store to buy some things. I always bought something to make it look legit, but I always had a lot of stuff under my skirt. He'd wait for me outside with our now three children. That day, after paying the cashier, I left as usual. In seconds, I was surrounded by several patrol cars, cops with guns drawn; they pushed me against one of the cars and cuffed me. Out of the corner of my eye, I saw him pull out of his parking spot and speed away. They took me to the police station, where they found everything. What's worse is that my cousin told me that he fled to the other side of the border with the children. I lost everything to that useless man! Now I think I'll never see my kids again. He's taken them too." We could argue as to whether she was a victim or an accomplice, or both. Truth is, she lost everything for falling in love with a thief, a liar, and abuser.

This truth brings to memory another greater and more important truth. A wonderful person lost everything for loving liars, thieves, and abusers—in short, sinners. The apostle Paul wrote about Jesus, "who, existing in the form of God, did not consider equality with God as something to be exploited. Instead, he emptied himself by assuming the form of a servant, taking on the likeness of humanity. And when he had come as a man, he humbled himself by becoming obedient to the point of death—even to death on a cross" (Philippians 2:6-8). In fact, these words were used in one of the first worship songs of the newly born Christian community. Jesus Christ emptied himself of his glory and all that surrounded his divine being. But he did not just empty himself. He then chose to wrap himself in human flesh and take on himself everything that is ours: our imperfection, defects, our thievery and hypocrisy . . . in short, our sin. That is good news for all big and little thieves, and their accomplices. As proof, he was crucified between two thieves. Thus, he cleansed all thieves by taking the guilt of their thievery on himself. Further, by justifying them, the ungodly, he restored all they had taken from the glory of God.

We don't need to just point the finger to people such as the couple in our story, pretending we are "squeaky clean." We do the same thing with members of our families. We rob them of the time and affection we could give our children and spouse, and spend it on useless and worthless things—and relationships. Then, when we don't love God with "all our heart, soul, and mind" and tune our lives to this law of love, we rob him of the honor God deserves as our Creator.

But because he loved us unto death, entering our jail house of a planet, full of thieves and sinners, "Therefore God also highly exalted him and gave him the name that is above every name, so that at the name of Jesus every knee will bow, in heaven and on earth and under the earth, and every tongue will confess that Jesus Christ is Lord, to the glory of God the Father" (Philippians 2:9-11, EHV). But that confession will not be made apart from him, but together with him. Because by grace alone, he fulfilled his promise that where he is, we will also be there with him. From thieves to glory, that's what he accomplished by loving us. He didn't lose all. Instead, he lost all to win us all by his infinite and unmerited grace! Now, let him steal your heart!

28

Live Wrestling In The Courtroom

> "But even more than that, I consider everything to be a loss because of what is worth far more: knowing Christ Jesus, my Lord. For his sake, I have lost all things and consider them rubbish, so that I may gain Christ" (Philippians 3:8, EHV).

"And, what does the mother say about these accusations?"

"Your Honor, it's all true. Regardless of what she was told last week, that she was on probation, that she had to go to school, that she couldn't leave the house after eight, she's been doing everything backwards! To top it off, we just found out this sixteen-year-old girl is already seven weeks pregnant! And she says she's not even sure who the father is!" The woman could no longer hold back her tears. At the defendant's stand, sitting next to her attorney, the girl was focused on her fingernails.

The probation officer spoke up. "There's more, Your Honor. This morning she gave a dirty test for marijuana. She needs to be locked up."

"I believe you're right," replied the judge matter-of-factly. "We better let her stay in juvenile hall for a while. We have to protect her as well as the little one she's carrying." As he spoke, the bailiff stood behind the young woman, quickly placed her hands behind her back, and proceeded to place her in handcuffs. But as soon as she felt the cold metal, she jumped up, pushed the bailiff away, took a couple of steps toward the door where there was another bailiff waiting. He tried to block the exit to prevent her from vaulting away. Finally, it took four bailiffs to wrestle her to the ground while trying not to injure her abdominal area. But she resisted, twisting and shrieking all kinds of street obscenities. They finally handcuffed her and took her from the courtroom. Slowly, her shrieks receded into the distance.

At times, this is our behavior before God and others. And God lets us throw our tantrums. But we hurt others and ourselves with our theatrics. Then, life's circumstances have a way of wrestling us down to the ground. We kick, scream, and shriek, twist around with anger in live wrestling against God. How absurd! To pretend to wrestle the omnipotent!

Scripture narrates the story of such a man. He had to be knocked off his high horse. "Now Saul was still breathing threats and murder against the disciples of the Lord. He went to the high priest and requested letters from him to the synagogues in Damascus, so that if he found any men or women who belonged to the Way, he might bring them as prisoners to Jerusalem. As he traveled and was nearing Damascus, a light from heaven suddenly flashed around him. Falling to the ground, he heard a voice saying to him, 'Saul, Saul, why are you persecuting me?'" (Acts 9:1-4, CSB).

Saul of Tarsus was an influential member of his religion. It was the controlling belief of the time. It ruled that only through certain ceremonies and prescribed acts you could be accepted before God. But the religious authorities controlled the message and the compliance. And it was never enough. They always announced that even their best efforts were not enough. Besides, compliance had a financial obligation attached. The more you paid, the more your works were worthy before God (according to them). It was good business for the existing religion and surrounding religions, for they were all compliance based. These religions are always financed through fear and intimidation of a vengeful God, who will mete out punishment on the disobedient and unrepentant. But what they threaten falsely is that by God's decree (meaning their own), those who don't finance their business enterprise will be punished by God (meaning them).

So, when Saul heard that there were those who were preaching that acceptance before God was through faith alone in a Messiah that died for their sins, and that people were leaving his religion to join this new Way, he threw a fit, much like that girl in the courtroom. He lost power and control over people's minds. They had to be hunted down and silenced to get rid of that dangerous new teaching, which threatened the entire religious institution. If more people believed in the Way, his institution would go bankrupt. Further, Saul and all his fellow religious politicians would lose their power.

In the middle of Saul's rage, "A light from heaven suddenly flashed around him" (Acts 9:3, CSB). This was not just physical light. This was "the true light that enlightens every man" (John 1:9, RSV). This was "the light that shines in the darkness, and the darkness has not overcome it" (John 1:5, ESV). This was the light of the Way, the very light Saul was persecuting. The person he was persecuting was the light that stopped him cold in his tantrum with the very truth he was persecuting: that sinners are made right and justified before God through Christ alone, and by faith alone. The truth suddenly was so bright, that it blinded him to his own truth, to his own doctrine, to all that he held dear. Suddenly, he was spiritually bankrupt and had nothing to offer God, not even his own name, for he quickly changed it from Saul (king) to Paul (the little one). He just basked in the light that had blinded him. This is the light that cuts short human rebellion through the power of God's grace. It brings sinners to the light of faith alone, in Christ alone, through grace alone. And that's enough to knock anyone down and raise him up with Christ into heavenly places!

29

Mother vs. Grandmother

> "You must not fear, for I am with you; you must not be afraid, for I am your God. I will strengthen you, indeed I will help you, indeed I will take hold of you with the right hand of my salvation" (Isaiah 41:10, LEB). "I give them eternal life, and they will never perish. No one will snatch them out of my hand" (John 10:28, ESV).

Today the judge would issue his ruling in the custody of a six-year-old girl. On the one hand, the girl's biological mother had filed for full custody. On the other, the girl's paternal grandmother opposed the claim and had filed her own petition for full custody. But, where was the dad? The file read, "Whereabouts Unknown." Not even the dad's mother (the grandmother above) knew the whereabouts of her son. But before the father's disappearing act, the girl's mother had taken a trip to her own country, leaving the dad caring for the daughter. But the dad took advantage of her absence and requested full custody of his daughter. He argued that the mother had abandoned the home and was now living with another man in her own country. The judge granted the petition. Weeks later, the father disappeared, and his mother (the grandmother) had to care for the little girl. When the mother came back, the grandmother did not let the girl go back with her mother claiming that the judge had given full custody to her son, the girl's father. The grandmother's attorney alleged that the girl would suffer emotional injury if she went back with her mother, for she had already bonded with her grandmother.

The mother alleged that the girl would suffer injury if she stayed with the grandmother. She alleged that other adult men lived there and partied with street girls all week long. She feared that the daughter would be sexually abused in that environment. The judge granted full custody to the mother since the law gives priority to the parents and not to the grandparents. As she left the courtroom, the mother kept thanking the judge, "Thank you, thank you, thank you, Your Honor, I am so thankful, thank you!"

I don't blame you if you didn't quite follow that. It was somewhat convoluted.

But our own custody before God is not complicated. Our heavenly Father has always claimed us as his children, and has never abandoned us. "I have loved you with an everlasting love; I have drawn you with unfailing kindness" (Jeremiah 31:3, NIV). "This is what the Lord says—the one who created you . . . and the one who formed you . . . Do not fear, for I have redeemed you; I have called you by your name; you are mine" (Isaiah 43:1, CSB). This promise needs to be embraced in the light of the cross. We were redeemed from all true accusations and fair condemnation through Christ's sacrifice in our place. Nothing else makes us his and puts us under God's custody. Anything we offer does not do it. Only Christ's perfect and complete work in our behalf makes us eternally his. That is why the next promise we find in Isaiah's text is true. It reveals the profound meaning of God's redeeming act in Christ: "When you cross through the waters, I will be with you. When you cross the rivers, they will not sweep you away. When you walk through fire, you will not be burned, and the flame will not set you on fire. Because I am the Lord your God, the Holy One of Israel, your Savior" (Isaiah 43:2-3, EHV). These promises assure us that because we have been redeemed through the work of Christ, the core of our faith will not be moved under any circumstance. The core of our faith will remain under the custody of Christ. Our faith is not guarded by our feelings or emotions of "feeling God's power in our lives." Instead, our faith is anchored and protected by Christ's work, which cannot be removed from history. No matter what happens to us, no matter what evil threatens to overwhelm our faith, Christ's work for us will remain intact. His forgiveness will not be taken away. It was poured out at the cross for us.

Those who don't trust in Christ's work of redemption alone are filing a petition for self-custody. Once we put any trust in any of our own works, no matter how loving and self-giving, we sabotage his work on our behalf. We diminish its effectiveness. And once diminished, his work is useless for us. When we mix together our works with the works of Christ, they cancel each other out.

Self-custody turns the promise around: "When we cross through the waters, we will swim on through. When the flash floods overtake us, we will push our way through the mud, boulders, stumps, and logs. When we walk through the fire, we will take the burns." This type of humanistic self-custody works until the undertow takes us down, or until the smoke and the flames choke and blind us. Besides, it's worthless for the weak and the sick, those who can't swim or run through flames. There are those who are ardent believers in self-custody. They believe that they are better off separated from anything that reminds them of God, or their origin in him. In fact, they deny they have any past, present, or future in God. But even so, God at the cross gave his life to win their custody. There he said, "It doesn't matter what you think or believe, or where you go, you will never flee from my presence. Even in your unbelief my Spirit reaches you, and claims you as mine (Psalm 139:7). At the cross I shed my blood to have you under my custody forever, and it was not a futile act. I will triumph over your life!" "You must not fear, for I am with you; you must not be afraid, for I am your God. I will strengthen you, indeed I will help you, indeed I will take hold of you with the right hand of my salvation" (Isaiah 41:10, LEB).

The enemy of our souls also wants our custody. He shoves in our face our anger, hatred, bitterness, envy, and lust. He claims we are just like him, and so he deserves to have our custody. He argues that we don't deserve to be children of God, and even less his grace and mercy. Those are God's gifts reserved for a special group that has never strayed from him. That we'll have to pay on this earth for our sins if ever God will look our way and see if we're worthy of his custody. But this enemy is also a liar and the father of lies. Truth is that Jesus Christ is God's strong man, who went into the strong man's house and at the cross, pulled us all out. At the resurrection, he drew us unto him and took us to the father's bosom. Since those are the works of Christ that cannot be undone, his promise is, "I give them eternal life, and they will never perish. No one will snatch them out of my hand" (John 10:28, CSB).

30

His Hand Shook Just Inches From My Throat

> "He was wounded for our transgressions, and he was crushed for our iniquities, and the punishment that made us whole was upon him, and by his bruises we are healed. All we like sheep have gone astray, we have turned, each of us, to his own way; and the Lord has laid on him the iniquity of us all" (Isaiah 53:5-6, ISV).

"His hand shook just inches from my throat. Just then, my eleven-year-old daughter came in and yelled, 'Dad, what are you doing? Let go of my mom!'" After more than thirty years interpreting in the courtrooms, I'm still moved by such witness accounts. On this occasion, the woman testified before the jury of the abuse from her drunken husband on that night. He had knocked her to the floor, held her down with his knee on her chest, pulled out a switchblade and threatened to kill her.

The witness continued quoting the man, "I know that as soon as I leave the house for work, you let other men into the house, and they have their way with you. Who are they?" Then the woman described that he'd overpower her while reeking of alcohol and sweat. The woman's words were sometimes lost among her sobs and tears. Some distance away at the defense table, the defendant, emotionless, looked away. Among the audience a woman, the defendant's lover, looked on with a scornful smile as if enjoying the woman's pain. "This happened more times than I can count with both hands, Your Honor," added the victim. "I tried to tell him that he had always been my only man. But he answered me by slapping me. Sometimes, the mark of his fingers would linger on my cheeks for days. That's how he thanked me for the seventeen years I put up with him, and the five children I gave him. But no more! It's over!"

The traumatic experience of this woman reminded me of another victim of physical and verbal abuse—Jesus the Christ, his torture and death by crucifixion. His body was violently violated with the Roman lash. His purity was offended with countless obscenities, slaps, mocking, and finally he was stripped of his clothing exposing him to shame. The soldiers, too, must have reeked of cheap wine, sweat, blood, and the filth on the soldiers' boots. This is obviously too descriptive, and some readers will want to turn the page. But it doesn't even begin to describe that horrendous scene. To push up on the pain level, the enemy mocked him: "If you are the Son of God, why do you allow all this abuse? Or, maybe what it means is that you've been abandoned by your 'Father.' Truth is, you are no Son of God at all. You're just an impostor, a faker. You wasted all your life teaching about love and that lie about turning the other cheek. Now look at yourself; you can't even defend yourself like a man, even less like the Son of God you claim to be. It's not too late; just shout out how wrong you were, that you want to make peace with the religious authorities, that you apologize for offending them, and you'll be let down from the cross. And then, serve them, didn't you teach about service, and going the second mile? Well, go the second mile, and come down from the cross. And your followers? Where are they? You don't even have anyone to defend you! Where are the multitudes you fed? Where is your movement? You've been left all alone. So many people know you, so many people who claim you healed them, but did you really? How come they're not here now to cheer you on? Now no one will step forward for you. Your whole life has been a total waste!"

The victims of abuse will more closely identify with the sufferings of Christ, and see that in a very unique way, Christ identifies with them. But that is as far as the comparison goes. Christ's suffering was redemptive. There's nothing redemptive about any other victim's abuse. No victim should understand their abuse as redemptive, or as deserved, or as "I had it coming to me." Neither should they blame themselves for their abuse. Neither is it God's will that any one should be abused, not even once. The victimizer needs to be immediately reported to the authorities, regardless of who he or she is, and regardless of the consequences. Civil law declares it a crime, and God's law prohibits it with the mandate, "You shall not kill." Any abuse is a prelude to murder, and as Jesus amplified the law, the hatred behind the blows is already homicide. The physical and emotional scars will be worn by the victim all life long, painful reminders that such abuse must never happen again. What's more, the memory cells will recall them at the least expected moments and bring back the pain. None of this is deserved nor does it redeem for any mistake or offense.

Only Christ's passion redeems. "He was wounded for our transgressions, and he was crushed for our iniquities, and the punishment that made us whole was upon him, and by his bruises we are healed. All we like sheep have gone astray, we have turned, each of us, to his own way; and the Lord has laid on him the iniquity of us all" (Isaiah 53:5-6, ISV). Then, "No more! It's over!" Claim your freedom from all your abusers and be sheltered under his wings.

31

The Legitimately Immoral Marriage

> "And be found in him, not having mine own righteousness, which is of the law, but that which is through the faith of Christ, the righteousness which is of God by faith" (Philippians 3:9, KJ21). "This is His name by which He will be called, 'The Lord Our Righteousness'" (Jeremiah 23:6).

"Your Honor, all I want from you is to tell this nobody that I don't want anything to do with him; that's why I divorced him!"

"But madam, you're asking for a restraining order. That puts the burden on you to convince me that you've been hurt, wounded, or threatened with death," retorted the judge.

"It's that he's always coming to my house, and in front of my family tells us that he's going to get all of us deported, that he's going to report us to the authorities, that we're nothing but a bunch of illegals. Then he shows up at my work and repeats all that to my employers!"

To which the judge responded, "But I still don't see the black and blues on your skin, lacerations, or any type of physical injury, and I don't hear a death threat."

"It's that for me; it's all that and more. I'm embarrassed to tell you, Your Honor."

"Well, I'm all ears. Tell me all about it."

Then she continued, "I married this man under the promise that he was only going to give me the immigration papers, but there would be no intimacy between us, or living together. But he broke the promise. He wanted me as his wife, no matter what. But I didn't want to—didn't like him, but then he would force himself on me! I don't want that man as a husband, lover, friend, or anything! I detest him! But now that I went and filed for divorce, he shows up saying he's going to report all of us to immigration. And it wasn't an empty threat either. One day, he did show up at our house with immigration, and now they're investigating all of us! He's terrorizing us. Tell him to go away . . . that I never again want to see him in my life!"

But it's difficult to empathize with the woman, isn't it? It's a risk she took, and when the chips fell, she lost the bet. The law technically protected the man's rights as a husband. There had been no signed pre-nuptial contract with any stipulations regarding intimacy or living arrangements. It had been a verbal agreement, and the woman could not provide proof of such a contract. The signed marriage certificate empowered the man's immoral behavior with the woman. Although the man was not acting outside the boundaries of the law, certainly there were higher moral values he was disregarding. For instance: respect, dignity, honor, and compassion.

In his situation, there was a higher morality than that prescribed by the law. But the marriage law, regardless of its presumed high moral standard, winked its eye at the man forcing himself on the woman. And then, it also winked at the man's vengeful act of reporting the woman and her family to the immigration authorities. As a citizen, he was within his right to denounce the woman and her family to immigration. But the law had nothing to say about his vengeful intentions.

It's difficult to see that higher morality. We don't easily desist of blaming the woman for her "immoral act" of entering into a fraudulent marriage just to get her immigration papers. The law also sided with his vengeful intent. "*She* should have seen the pickle she was getting into." "If *she* hadn't broken the law, *she* would not have gotten into such trouble. Serves *her* right!" That tends to be our rather smug judgment.

Jesus faced the same situation with the Pharisees. They were sticklers for the law, but they used it as cover for their immorality. Their murderous intent to get rid of him, to be specific. That is why Jesus called them on it: "For I tell you that unless your righteousness surpasses that of the Pharisees and the teachers of the law, you will certainly not enter the kingdom of heaven" (Matthew 5:20, NIV). We need to look beyond our smug judgments regarding our understanding of the law and our keeping the law to a higher morality, a higher righteousness by which God indeed will declare us righteous and citizens of his kingdom. But how do we attain it?

I wish we had a video clip of Jesus saying those words to those surrounding him. One clip would show him addressing the crowd with finger pointing menacingly at them: "Unless your righteousness surpasses that of the Pharisees and the teachers of the law, you will certainly not enter the kingdom of heaven." The Pharisees were strict law keepers, as were the scribes or teachers of the law. In this instance, Christ would be saying "Unless you keep the law more strictly than the most extreme in keeping it, there's no hope for you." But this would only be a morality on par with the highest demands of the law. However, it would not exceed it. In this case, Christ would not have been a Savior at all, but nothing other than a new and more demanding Moses.

Let's look at another video clip in our imagination. Here Jesus the Messiah addresses the crowd with the same words. But when he says "your righteousness," he does not point at them, but directs his hands to himself. As if saying, "I am your righteousness, and my righteousness exceeds and far surpasses any other righteousness. Believe it, my righteousness is your righteousness, and because it is a much higher moral righteousness, as the heavens are higher than the earth, you will enter the kingdom of heaven!" In this case, Christ presents himself as the only righteousness that exceeded the law. He went above and beyond the righteousness of the law through his transcendent love when he gave his life to bear our sins. His perfect righteousness substitutes for our imperfect righteousness. His death is our death. His resurrection is ours. And, "you are complete in him" (Colossians 2:10, NKJV).

It had to be one of these two scenes. In scene one, Jesus puts the burden of surpassing the morality of the law on us. In scene two, Jesus puts the burden of exceeding the law on himself. And what's more, he says he is our righteousness and gifts it to us by faith alone, his own faith. That's how it was revealed to the apostle Paul, for his wish is to "be found in him, not having my own righteousness, which is of the law, but that which is through the faith of Christ, the righteousness which is of God by faith" (Philippians 3:9, KJ21). That is also how it was revealed to the prophet Jeremiah. He prophesied of the Messiah, "This is His name by which He will be called, 'The Lord Our Righteousness'" (Jeremiah 23:6, NASB).

And what does the prophet say of us? "They will say of Me, 'Only in the Lord are righteousness and strength'" (Isaiah 45:24, NASB).

32

He Left Me In The Scorching Son With My Boy

> "The God who made the world and everything in it" . . . "bought us for God with [His] blood out of every tribe and language and people and nation" (Acts 17:24, NIV; Revelation 5:9, EHV).

The young couple had a five-year-old boy. But the husband, instead of embracing happiness in his wife and son, thought he'd find it in women, alcohol, and drugs. Besides, he thought he'd make some extra cash with a sale or two. But he was swindled in one of his sales, leaving him with a $20,000 USD debt to the trafficker, who did not hesitate to threaten him and his family. Fearing the worst, he traveled to the United States with his young family. But nothing changed with his change of venue. He was drinking more, and then for the slightest misunderstanding with his wife, he'd threaten to have her deported, and keep the child. It was a reign of terror: blows, verbal abuse, humiliations, rape. She pleaded with him to quit drinking. His answer was more violence and alcohol. Finally, one day in a fit of rage, he threw her out of the house. She had walked to the store and when she came back, he had locked her out. Outside the temperature in the hot desert valley was 111° F (44° C). "Stay out!" he yelled. "Now you're gonna get deported. The cops will find you; they'll accuse you of child endangerment, and you'll never again bother me!"

With only tears to quench her thirst, she walked down the scorching street. She remembered there was a fire station nearby. She decided to take her chances with them, but especially to protect her son. Once there, she told them what had happened. The emergency personnel called the police who immediately took her to a nearby shelter for battered women. Her worst nightmares never came true. She found shelter and grace where she least expected. She was further sheltered by a law that protects victims of abuse, by granting them immunity from deportation and putting them on the path to citizenship. Her worst fears turned into an unexpected blessing. In turn, the man was arrested for child abuse and endangerment, the police found links to his drug trafficking and sent him to federal prison for ten years to be followed with a deportation order.

Scripture relates that Abraham, the father of faith, in a huge lapse of faith, conceived Ishmael with Hagar, his wife's servant. God had promised Abraham an heir, but with Sarah, his wife, not her servant. But both Sarah and Abraham did not trust in God's promise—too impossible to come true at their age—and came up with the Hagar affair. But Scripture says, "Everything that isn't based on faith is sin" (Romans 14:23, CEB). In this case, that lack of faith almost destroyed their home. Sarah's infertility did not go away, and the child from that affair did not bring them the expected happiness. Things were going from bad to worse: jealousies, humiliations, resentments, scorn, mockery. Until one day, Sarah told Abraham, "Look, it's either her or me!" Abraham listened to Sarah's claim and with a broken heart sent Hagar away with her son, Ishmael. They were left homeless in the scorching heat of the Palestinian desert. Scripture narrates the account.

> Abraham got up early in the morning. He took bread and a waterskin, which he gave to Hagar, putting it over her shoulder. He sent her away with her child. She set out and wandered in the wilderness near Beersheba. The water in the skin was used up, and she dragged the child under one of the bushes. She went and sat down by herself, across from him, at a distance, about a bow shot away, because she said, "Do not let me see the death of the child." She sat across from him and wept loudly. God heard the boy's voice, and the Angel of God called to Hagar out of heaven and said to her, "What is wrong, Hagar? Do

> not be afraid, for God has heard the boy's voice right where he is. Get up. Help the boy up, and take him by the hand because I will make him into a great nation." (Genesis 21:14-18, EHV).

God's mercy and grace also reaches out to the children of faithlessness and sin, the abandoned, the rejected, humiliated, dispossessed, spurned, banished, and the exiled: those who hunger and thirst after righteousness. God hears the cry of these children and their parents. "The God who made the world and everything in it" . . . "bought us for God with [His] blood out of every tribe and language and people and nation" (Acts 17:24, NIV; Revelation 5:9, EHV). Take courage in the valley of your scorching shade-less desert. You and yours have been redeemed and taken under the wing of God's family and forever!

33

I'm Ashamed To Say What I Let Him Do

> "Father, forgive them, for they know not what they do" (Luke 23:34, KJ21). "He was numbered with the transgressors; and He bore the sin of many, and made intercession for the transgressors" (Isaiah 53:12, KJ21).

On a certain day, a woman appeared before the judge requesting a restraining order against her husband. Timidly, she answered the judge's questions detailing the two times when he had assaulted her. "Two years ago he shoved me against a car engine there in the garage. I cut my scalp, and they sewed me up with five stitches. This last time was when he got home; he saw me talking on the phone. He yanked the phone from my hand and slapped me so hard I hit the floor." Her voice would fade amid her sobs. The judge then asked the husband to respond to those allegations.

"About the engine, we were arguing; she lunged at me. I ducked, and she fell against the engine. That's not my fault."

At that moment, something caught my attention. The woman's hands were trembling on her lap under the table. The husband continued, "About the slap, that's a big lie. Yes, she was talking on the phone instead of coming out to greet me. It's my phone; I only went to retrieve it, and yes, I took it from her hands." The woman's hands were trembling even more as she rubbed them against each other. The judge issued the restraining order, and we left the courtroom.

Once outside, the woman said, "Excuse me that my hands were shaking so much."

"But tell me, why?"

"It's that I told the judge a lie."

"Really?" I questioned.

"Yes."

"But why?"

"It's because he didn't hit me just those two times. It's been so many, I lost count. Finally, I got tired, and that's why I called the police."

"But why didn't you tell the judge?"

"It's because I'm ashamed to tell everything I let that man do to me!"

Unfortunately, this story is repeated many times in victims of spousal abuse. Often times, it's too late for the victims, and they die at the hands of their spouse. The law provides restraining orders, which offers some protection, and they are available to all.

It is evident that the gospel narrations of Christ's physical suffering at the hands of the Roman tormentors and then at his crucifixion, do not tell the whole story. Indeed, the whole story has not been told, and will not be known – at least for now.

There are many scientific accounts that attempt to recreate the sufferings of Jesus both at the flogging post in Pilate's courtyard, then on the Via Dolorosa, and finally on the cross at Calvary. Yet only the Christ himself knows what he went through, and chose not to reveal the entire account of his sufferings. Had it been necessary for our salvation, he would have revealed them all. To be aware of his physical sufferings would not lead us to faith but to pity. And pity is not of faith. Pity leads to disdain, or at best, sympathy. But not faith.

After his resurrection, Christ did give an account of his sufferings that does lead to faith. It is found in Luke 24. But what stands out is not what he felt, or how he overcame the pain. Jesus's focus is on the meaning of his suffering and death, for it is the meaning of what he did that leads to faith. "He said to them, 'This is what I told you while I was still with you: Everything must be fulfilled that is written about me in the Law of Moses, the Prophets and the Psalms.' Then he opened their minds so they could understand the Scriptures. He told them, "This is what is written: The Messiah will suffer and rise from the dead on the third day, and repentance for the forgiveness of sins will be preached in his name to all nations" (Luke 24:44-47, NIV).

So it's not about how he suffered. It's about *why* he suffered. It was to give us "repentance for the forgiveness of sins."

Wait a minute. That phrase doesn't quite make sense. According to our logic, it should be "repentance so that your sins will be forgiven." Or, "your sins will be forgiven *if* you repent. But "repentance for the forgiveness of sins" sounds like repentance is given to us *because* of his sufferings. He suffered to give us repentance. But, repentance from what? Repentance from believing our sins are too big and too numerous to be forgiven. Repentance from believing we don't deserve to be forgiven. Repentance from thinking there is no Good News for us. Repentance from thinking that because our sins are too outrageous, we need to do outrageous things to pay for them.

But what does repentance mean? In New Testament Greek, the word is *metanoia*. One of the literal meanings is "beyond what you're thinking." Repentance means to think way beyond what you've been thinking about what God in Christ has done for you. It means to think beyond what you've been thinking, and then believe that you will find repentance in his sufferings, and not in your works of penitence. But, why? How does it work?

Let the Scriptures themselves explain. "But he was pierced for our transgressions, he was crushed for our iniquities; the punishment that brought us peace was on him, and by his wounds we are healed. We all, like sheep, have gone astray, each of us has turned to our own way; and the Lord has laid on him the iniquity of us all" (Isaiah 53:5-6, NIV). "For the transgression of my people he was punished" (v. 8). "The Lord makes his life an offering for sin" (v. 10). "He was numbered among the transgressors, for he bore the sin of many, and made intercession for the transgressors" (v. 12).

How did that happen? How was our iniquity placed on him? We don't know. God will keep that mystery. But we are told that our iniquity and its eternal consequences were placed on him. His suffering was for "the transgression of his people." Think of it. His people transgress. He lifted their transgression, their sins and shortcomings, and placed them all on him. He made his life an offering for sin, replacing all the sin offerings of the Old Testament, all sin offerings anyone could ever offer throughout human history. He bore the sin of a countless "many." His sufferings were vicarious, in lieu of . . . in our place. We had nothing to do with the forgiveness of our sins. Neither can we alter or in any way change what he did to forgive us.

That is how his suffering generates faith and repentance in us, assuring us that our sins were forgiven at the cross. But what's more, we as the human beings we are, the entire package of our lives, from birth to death, has been eternally forgiven.

It's not pity. We've been conquered by faith in his sufferings, and we're not ashamed to tell all that he's done for us.

34

I Made Up The Whole Story

"This is love: not that we loved God, but that he loved us and sent his Son as an atoning sacrifice for our sins. Dear friends, since God so loved us, we also ought to love one another" (1 John 4:10-11, NIV).

The man looked much older than his fifty years. Frail and fragile, he moved and talked as if he were decades older. In his jail orange jump suit, handcuffed and shackled, he looked even more helpless and vulnerable. It was difficult to understand his half-muttered speech. "I didn't do anything of what they accuse me. It's all a misunderstanding. Talk again to my wife and the girl. She was the one who assaulted me."

The police report contained the opposite. It claimed that when they arrived, the fifteen-year-old girl was furious. She told them that her father had shoved her against the wall, hit her face with a closed fist, and then struck her with a broomstick several times over the head. These were serious accusations, charged as felonies, with a weapon enhancement (the broomstick). The police arrested the man even though the young woman showed no marks of the alleged blows. Weeks later, now appearing for jury trial, the defendant was facing many years in the state penitentiary.

As we waited, a woman approached me and said she wanted to talk to the district attorney. Beside her was a young woman dressed in jeans and a sweater. She spoke first.

"I'm the one you call the victim," she said. "But things didn't happen the way it says in the police report. I was the one who assaulted my dad. It's that I didn't want to clean up my room. I got mad at him 'cause he was bugging me about it. I made up the whole story to get him off my back. But now I'm sorry for what I did. I told a big lie. The cops have no proof. They didn't take pictures of me or anything because nothing happened to me."

At the end of trial, it was a hung jury. They were not convinced. They could not declare him guilty or not guilty. The judge declared a mistrial. But immediately, the district attorney said they were filing charges once again and announced a retrial. The young woman covered her face with her hands while her body shook as she helplessly tried to control her crying. "I'm so bad, I'm so bad," she repeated.

But many other times, the victims of physical and/or sexual abuse have not made up anything. All their accusations are true. But they attempt to retract them when they see the grave consequences to the perpetrator, especially if he is a family member. On the other hand, there are presumed victims who have made false accusations. When they see the harm they have caused their father, or uncle, or grandfather, in vain do they try to retract their accounts. Many times, people are falsely accused and condemned, even to a life sentence for crimes they never committed.

At the heavenly court, all accusations against us are true. These are not the charges brought against us by Satan, the father of lies. His charges always contain half-truths about us, either exaggerating our bad deeds, or inflating our good ones. But the true charges are brought about by God's law, particularly regarding the summary of the law: "You must love the Lord your God with all your heart, with all your soul, and with all your mind. This is the greatest and most important commandment. The second is exactly like it: You must love your neighbor as yourself" (Matthew 22:37-39, ISV). But if we summarize the summary, the accusations are undeniable. "You must live this way: Love God, love neighbor."

Love God? How do we even know what that looks like? Or what that feels like? Or how do we measure it? How much love for God is needed? How can we love someone we cannot see and touch? How do we love God with all our heart, if our heart is deceitful and desperately wicked? (Jeremiah 17:9). What about our soul, if it is born in sins and trespasses? And what about our mind, since like the antediluvians "every imagination of the thoughts of [our] heart is only evil continually"? (Genesis 6:5, ASV). When we truly understand the command to love God and neighbor, we ask with the psalmist, "If you, Lord, kept a record of sins, Lord, who could stand?" (Psalm 130:3, NIV). Or, with Paul, "And who is sufficient for these things?" (2 Corinthians 2:16, ASV). Or plea with David, "Don't try me in your court, because no one is innocent by your standards" (Psalm 143:2, CEV).

Christ said to Philip, "He who has seen me has seen the Father" (John 14:9, MEV). We cannot come close to loving God without knowing and seeing Christ. God cannot be truly loved apart from Christ. Scripture says, "God was in Christ reconciling the world to Himself, not counting people's sins against them" (2 Corinthians 5:19, AMP). The apostle John makes it personal: "This is love: not that we loved God, but that he loved us and sent his Son as an atoning sacrifice for our sins. Dear friends, since God so loved us, we also ought to love one another. No one has ever seen God; but if we love one another, God lives in us and his love is made complete in us . . . We love because he first loved us" (1 John 4:10,11,19, NIV). We love God as we see Christ bearing our sins and pouring out his life for us. Then at the resurrection, taking us up into himself, and into the presence of the Father. This is when human love for God begins to awaken in the heart. And then we turn toward our neighbor with the same love and compassion. We cannot love our neighbor apart from the mercy shown to us on the cross.

But even so, our love for Christ and neighbor will always be defective. In order to fulfill the commandment, we must always claim Christ's love for us as our own. The command to love God and neighbor is only fulfilled by faith alone in the fullness of Christ's love for us. He was the love of God in its very essence while on earth. And by grace, his love is fully counted as our own. The girl in our story covered her face with regret repeating, "I'm so bad, I'm so bad." But God's loving arm embraces us and tells us to repeat: "I'm loved, I've been forgiven!"

35

My Mother Needed Heart Surgery

> "The Lord is my shepherd, I shall not want," for "my God will supply every need of yours according to his riches in glory in Christ Jesus" (Psalm 23:1; Philippians 4:19, ESV).

The bus had just crossed the border. Minutes later, it arrived at the station. As the passengers disembarked, the border patrol was waiting with contraband detection dogs. The canines were slowly sniffing at the passengers and their baggage. One of the hounds became interested in the two suitcases of a twenty-two-year-old man, then sat next to them signaling a positive find. Another hound stood in front of the young man blocking his way. A couple of agents approached from behind, spoke briefly with him, and took him to an interview room. After checking his personal documents, he was told to open the suitcases. He moved the clothes from one side to another, but the expert eye of a narcotics agent detected the shine of cellophane paper. Taking the clothes out of the suitcase, the agent found three cakes of heroin and two in the other suitcase. It was a total of five and a half kilos (almost twelve pounds). He was then taken to the police station where he was booked, and then sent to jail. Today he was appearing in court answering to charges of illegal transport of a prohibited substance with a weight enhancement greater than four kilos. His public defender instructed him that he was facing eight to ten years in federal prison.

He then asked if he had any defense for his actions. "We live in poverty. My mother needs open heart surgery. We don't have medical insurance. No one could help us. An acquaintance told me about these guys. They just told me to take the baggage to the other side where they would pay me $100,000 dollars, which would cover the surgery costs. They didn't even tell me it was drugs. Don't you understand my need?"

The court never found out if the man's mother really needed heart surgery, or if it was an alibi. It didn't need to. What the law knew was that he was transporting five and a half kilos of heroin. The district attorney assumed it was for sales. The law didn't care about the claim of his mother's surgery. His public defender's comments were terse: "You got nailed by five pounds of heroin and two hound dogs."

At the heavenly courtroom, the evidence of our sins and the hound dog of the law have nailed us. God's law doesn't care about our alibis for sin. It doesn't take into account the reasons for our good deeds, or the pretexts for the bad ones. What we have inside is sin and rebellion, and God's law; the divine hound dog sniffs it out. "For the word of God is alive and active. Sharper than any double-edged sword, it penetrates even to dividing soul and spirit, joints and marrow; it judges the thoughts and attitudes of the heart" (Hebrews 4:12, NIV). It sniffs out everything that is not of faith, and charges it as sin (Romans 14:23). Sin is a word that today – quite conveniently – has come into disuse. It is not politically correct to call anything sin. It raises the specter of guilt, shame, and all that society sweeps under its moral carpet as useless.. Society claims that the concept of sin is debilitating and derails the full potential of human capacity to be fully one's self and be free to accomplish great and wonderful deeds. As we look around, we may safely ask, "How far has that claim gotten us today?" The great hound dog of heaven sniffs out our "full potential," our "capacity for transformation and transforming," and found it lacking. Even our best intentions are toxic with sin. Like the great finger that wrote on the wall of Belshazzar's palace, the same finger writes all over our best (and worst) social media sites: "You have been weighed on the scales and found wanting" (Daniel 5:27, NIV).

But seeing that we were to be nailed to a hopeless future by our sins, there was one who took hold of those nails just in time, and made them his. He was nailed in our place by the burden of our sins, and the heavenly hound dog of God's law. This is our other great reality. In him we were condemned to an eternal prison. In his resurrection we were freed. He is the true fulfillment of the original human capacity and found complete. And all that is his is ours by faith alone. Yes, God understands our supreme need for forgiveness and righteousness, and has already fully provided for all our needs in Christ. "He who did not spare his own Son, but gave him up for us all—how will he not also, along with him, graciously give us all things?" (Romans 8:32, NIVUK). So confess it, that reality is yours today. "The Lord is my shepherd, I shall not want," for "my God will supply every need of yours according to his riches in glory in Christ Jesus" (Psalm 23:1; Philippians 4:19, ESV).

36

The Weapons Remind Him of His Father

> "I give them eternal life, and they will never perish. No one will snatch them out of my hand. My Father, who has given them to me, is greater than all. No one can snatch them out of my Father's hand" (John 10:28-29, EHV).

"So tell me in a few words why you want to change the names of your three children. They're growing up; they can wait until they're eighteen and do it themselves if they want to," instructed the judge.

"It's a long story, Your Honor. I don't know if you have the time," responded the mother.

"Try to make it brief," said the judge, already showing his impatience. But soon he wasn't even blinking.

"I didn't know that the man with whom I fell in love was trafficking in drugs when I went to live with him. He dazzled me with his own house, and it was huge. There was a beautiful swimming pool, Jacuzzi, jewelry, cars, and maids. He told me he was a businessman and had his own import and export business. He was quite older; I had just turned eighteen. We met at a friend's birthday party. I didn't think twice about it. But soon I was pregnant. In three years, I had three children.

Then he told me I was useless, that I wasn't the same as before. We argued about everything. He spent a lot of time at his other house, which was next door. He prohibited us from setting a foot near the house. One night, when my youngest was seven years old, out of curiosity he went next door, found an open door, and came back running. He told me there were bad things happening in the living room. That there was a man tied to a chair, with something in his mouth; and that his dad was shouting bad words at him, holding a gun over his head. I ran over to see for myself and saw worse things. It seems he also trafficked in young women. That same night I picked up my children, gathered a few things, and left the house. Now eight years later that boy is fascinated with weapons. All he talks about is weapons and what he could do with them. He says the weapons remind him of his father's name."

"I think I now understand why you want to change their names, lady," replied the judge. "You think that if you change the children's names, they will forget him."

"That's right, Your Honor."

The judge briefly placed his hand on his forehead, and looked the other way, obviously moved by the story. "Your children need more than a name change, madam," he responded.

"And what would that be, Your Honor?"

The judge paused briefly as if trying to find the right words. Then, he concluded, "They need a new father, madam. They need a new father, and it may be too late for that . . ."

Such is our own situation. We are sinners—fakers. We'd rather dazzle with who we are not, in order to hide who we really are. Our old father is an expert at dazzling and faking love, but short on delivering true love. That is why we need a new father. And it's never too late for that.

On a certain occasion, Jesus described the true human condition. "You are of your father the devil, and you want to do the desires of your father. He was a murderer from the beginning, and does not stand in the truth, because there is no truth in him. When he lies, he speaks from his own nature, for he is a liar and the father of lies" (John 8:44, MEV). Those are strong words. You would think Jesus was speaking to a gathering of pagans. But here he was speaking to the most religious people of his time, but who were planning to kill him. Talk about living a lie! While you pretend to be religious and a leader, secretly, you are planning murder. They were indeed children of the devil, in whom there is no truth. If we had access to the devil's moral gauge, the truth marker would be at zero! Nothing of what he sells, insinuates, and tempts with, has one millionth of truth!

That is indeed why we need another father. We have imprinted in our minds the lies of the devil. So, we need a new father. And indeed we have one, through Christ, who became our brother so that we may have his same Father. And just as there is not one millionth of truth in the devil, so there is not one millionth of a lie in the Father and the Son. When Jesus said, "The Father himself loves you" (John 16:27, CEB), he was saying that God's love for us doesn't have the smallest atomic particle of disdain for us. All of God's heart is nothing but love for us. But the funnel into the Father's heart is through the Son, our brother, Jesus Christ. He confirmed that when he taught us to pray, "Our father, who art in Heaven" (Matthew 6:9, KJ21). Then he added, "No one comes to the Father except through me" (John 14:6, ESV). Jesus is the way to the Father's heart. Not because the Father is exclusive and doesn't want us to know him directly; it's that we'll get a wrong idea of who he is apart from Christ. For "God was in Christ reconciling the world unto himself" (2 Corinthians 5:19, ASV). At the cross, we find out the true nature of the Father's heart, who brings us back to himself with a gift outside of us. That gift is found in the person of Christ, whose life, death, and resurrection are counted as our very own. In that gift, we know the Father's heart toward us.

When by faith we have grasped the Son, we have been taken into the Father's bosom, and in Father and Son we are loved and held eternally. "I give them eternal life, and they will never perish. No one will snatch them out of my hand. My Father, who has given them to me, is greater than all. No one can snatch them out of my Father's hand" (John 10:28-29, EHV).

Before, much like the boy in our story, we were fascinated with the weapons of our other father, the liar. He had seduced us with his grandiose claims of who he was—and his weapons: hatred, lust, anger, and greed.

But our heavenly Father has won our hearts with nothing but his love. A love that took him to the cross as well, for in the darkness of Calvary, God was present in the Son, bringing the entire creation back to himself.

So we have a Father, a dad, who cares for us more deeply than we could ever know or understand. It's never too late for us. It's never been too late. Even before the foundation of the world, we already had our Dad.

37

Look For The Face of God

> "But in keeping with his promise we are looking forward to a new heaven and new earth where of the first things there won't be any memory, neither will it come into our thoughts . . . where only righteousness dwells" (2 Peter 3:13; Isaiah 65:17, NIV).

"This letter was confiscated from a lockup in his jail cell. We believe it contains ciphered information about his plans for escape. It was written by his mother. We believe it has the code about the person who is going to help him break out. We need you to translate it so we can use it as evidence and prevent the escape."

The agents handed me two hand-written sheets with large and uneven letters. The spelling was horrible. By the contents, it was a mother writing to her son behind bars. I began translating and soon read the paragraph of interest to the investigators.

"We have the faith that you will be out soon. Take the hand of God. God will lead you out. Look for the face of God. God's face is the face of the person who will help you. He will lead your way to freedom. Remember that no matter what happens, your mother will always love you. I hope to see you soon."

"There, that's it, that's the part of interest to us," said the detective. "We want to question the inmate about his escape plan. Obviously, his mother has gotten someone to help him, most likely someone from the inside. We have to stop this plan before they try it. He must be a jail employee or even one of the deputies who's an accomplice."

I could not hide a knowing smile. I translated the paragraph again. As I handed the sheet back to them, I said, "Good luck. You are dealing with a mother's faith in God and her prayers. The only thing you'll find is the heart of a mother who won't stop loving her son."

"Yeah, right" they shot back. "You don't know the huge crimes this guy has committed." But neither did they know the huge size of a mother's heart.

"He who has seen me, has seen the Father," said Jesus (John 14:9, MEV). But he was talking about looking at him hanging from the cross. The mother of our story was right. We can look at God in the face of whoever helps us when we least expect it. Even so, it's a blurred reflection of the reality we see when we see Christ carrying our sins on his own body. No one has ever helped us so greatly as when Jesus took our guilt and condemnation on his own flesh. Yes, it was he who from the "inside" of our jail led us to freedom. When he took our place and suffered the "wages of sin" for every sinner, he opened the door of eternal life for us. Because until then, we were dead in our trespasses and sins (Ephesians 2:1). He was that "Fifth Columnist," that "Trojan Horse" sent from the Father, who became human flesh to remove the death sentence hanging over us by taking it upon himself. He was, and is still today, our "break out plan."

Of course, there are many who could care if God exists or not, or if we are indeed caught up in our sins and trespasses, or captive in anyway. They see their captivity to death as freedom to be whoever they want to be. But they are indeed bound to the jail of whoever they already are. That they cannot escape. They do not care if Christ really was a historical figure or not. They would rather assign him to the mythical figure category. They don't care to be rescued because they don't think they are bound. Yet, they are the same who seek to work their way out of their own dilemmas, whether they are personal relationship struggles or how to bring down the temperature of the earth a couple of degrees, or find an exoplanet in another solar system where someday humanity may escape.

But regardless of all doubt, the doubts of the greatest doubters cannot erase the truth. There is life eternal, and we were created to have it and to have it more abundantly (John 10:10). We really don't know the size of our Father's heart. And no one gets there except through Christ. He is our only plan of escape to that "new heaven and new earth where of the first things there won't be any memory, neither will it come into our thoughts . . . where only righteousness dwells" (Isaiah 65:17; 2 Peter 3:13, NIV). If we don't believe it, it's because we have no idea how great is the love in God's heart for us, but it will be slowly revealed to us. And in spite of our unbelief, the love of the Father will work his way into our hearts until we are free from the grave of our unbelief.

38

He Was Born Addicted To Methanphetamine

> "Can a mother forget the baby at her breast and have no compassion on the child she has borne? Though she may forget, I will not forget you!" (Isaiah 49:15, NIV). "Do not fear, for I have redeemed you; I have summoned you by name; you are mine" (Isaiah 43:1, NIV).

As soon as the baby was born, he was tested for drugs. A couple of hours after anxious waiting, the doctor's announcement devastated the mother: "Your son was born addicted to methamphetamine. We've already reported the situation to the authorities. They're on their way to take custody of the baby. We cannot let you care for him. The blood sample that we took from you also tested positive for cocaine, marijuana, and opioids. You also tested positive for blood alcohol. You were drinking a few hours before giving birth. The newborn will suffer strong withdrawal symptoms."

The mother's scream at the delivery room was heart wrenching. But it was no longer due to birth pains, but for the pain of not being able to hold her newborn son. Now, a month later, she was again in labor, giving birth to the legal consequences of her addictions in a courtroom before the judge. "Lady, there are no words to describe your crime. There's no way to predict the consequences that you've brought on that child for the rest of his life. But you should be very thankful for your husband. From the moment the baby was born, he's taken charge of the boy and cared for him every minute. The child has literally been in his father's hands. The baby had very strong withdrawal symptoms during the first five days, but due to your husband's constant care, he's out of danger. But you, young lady, are just beginning to face the consequences. You are not out of danger. If within the next six months you don't overcome your addictions, my ruling will remove your parental rights as long as he's a minor. You will lose all your rights as the mother of this child."

Our situation before God is quite similar. We arrive in this world already addicted to sin. As the ancient antediluvians, our thoughts and the imagination of our hearts always leans toward evil—in all its shapes and forms. Our first parents drank deep from the drugs of rebellion, selfishness, pride, and lying. We emerge infected.

But the Father, because of the great love with which he loved us, ran to us. He took us in his arms and placed us in the manger with his Son. Tenderly, he placed all broken humanity within him. We grew up in Christ's purity, innocence, and affection. Jesus's childhood was mine. His teenage years were mine—his youth and early adulthood as well. His entire life was mine. His death was my death. His rising from the dead and emerging from the tomb were mine. In him, we were all made new and rescued. In his resurrection, we were all born anew, a new creation in him. "Can a mother forget the baby at her breast and have no compassion on the child she has borne? Though she may forget, I will not forget you!" (Isaiah 49:15, NIV). In Jesus Christ, the Father became incarnate mercy to us and for us. "Do not fear, for I have redeemed you; I have summoned you by name; you are mine" (Isaiah 43:1, NIV).

It doesn't matter what your past has been or what your present looks like, or how afraid you are of your future. These promises are for you: "I give them eternal life. They will never die, and no one will snatch them from my hand. My Father, who has given them to me, is greater than anyone. No one can steal them out of my Father's hand" (John 10:28-29, EHV). This is indeed intensive care and recovery for all born under the addiction of sin. We are found somewhere in that pile, and he calls us by our name. The worst sinners answer first. Those who think they are not in that pile answer last. Yet, they also answer when they realize they are addicted to themselves.

In Christ's life, we are all rescued from the pile. The promises of Scripture light up faith in us. And even if you don't feel it, don't panic. Saving faith does not necessarily ravish with emotion. Saving faith is also a silent grasp of the Father's hand, as a newborn grasps unto his Father's little finger. And from there nothing nor anyone will ever snatch you away! (John 10:29).

39

Your Accuser Is A No Show, Case Dismissed

> Jesus stood up and said to her, "Woman, where are they? Is there no one to condemn you?" She said, "No one, sir." Jesus said, "Neither do I condemn you. Go, and from now on, don't sin anymore" (John 8:10-11, CEB).

The attorney advised his client: "Look lady, today I'm going to plead you not guilty before the judge."

"But I did run the stop light," she answered.

"Don't worry, madam. I'm your attorney. What you have is called 'consciousness of guilty,' but before you are declared guilty of any crime, the accuser has to show up and present the evidence. In this case, if the cop, who is your accuser, doesn't show up for trial, or if his evidence doesn't convince the judge, the judge has to dismiss the charges."

"Well, I don't quite understand all that," answered the woman.

"Let's see if my plan works," responded the lawyer with a knowing smile. Then he added, "If on trial day the police agent that accuses you of this infraction doesn't show up, the judge is obligated to dismiss the case."

The lady still moved her head from side to side signaling that she didn't understand. "As for today, I will plead you not guilty before the judge. Then I will ask for a trial date. In almost 55 percent of all cases, the cops don't show up."

Weeks later, I saw the woman come into court with her attorney. When the court clerk called out the police agent's name, the lawyer quickly winked at his client. Then, when the judge called the woman's name he said, "Lady, your accuser is a no show. Case dismissed; you may leave the courtroom." The woman opened her mouth as if to say something, but the lawyer signaled her to keep quiet. Still open mouthed, but with a huge smile, she followed her lawyer out of the courtroom.

On a certain occasion, a select group of religious leaders brought a woman before Jesus. They had been secretly deceiving and abusing her, but accused her of adultery. "'Teacher,' they said to him, 'this woman was caught in the act of committing adultery. In the Law, Moses commanded us to stone such women. So what do you say?'" (John 8:4-5, ESV). But Jesus was already aware of her guilt and didn't need any evidence against her.

But when they accused her as guilty, they were doing nothing else but accusing themselves, because they had not brought along the man with whom she allegedly had committed adultery. If they had surprised her "in the act" where was the man? The law required the man's presence as well. Since obviously they were covering up for him, they themselves were complicit. So Jesus confronted them with the evidence of their guilt. He began listing them on the sand. Names of their lovers. Dates. Places. One by one they scurried away, dropping the stones intended for the woman as they left until no one was left. Finally, Jesus asked the woman, "Where are your accusers? Did no one condemn you?"

She answered, "No one, Lord."

"Case dismissed. There are no accusers. Go in peace. Be careful; don't sin anymore [you don't know what they might do to you next time]. But neither do I condemn you" (John 8:4-11).

But if she was guilty, why didn't he condemn her? Because he himself carried her guilt on his body. With that guilt, he climbed up on the cross; he condemned himself for her sin and ours as well. That is the Good News of the Gospel. The only one who could condemn us took our guilt and sentence upon himself. Why? Because he loves us. Looking upon that wonder, the apostle Paul exclaimed, "If God be for us, who can be against us?" (Romans 8:31, ESV). But what of that select group of religious leaders who were ready to stone her to death? They left Jesus standing. They took off. Why didn't they also fall at Jesus's feet declaring him Lord and pleading for his mercy?

When there is no accuser, there is no condemnation. But when you're giving away pardons, and the guilty take flight, who is there to forgive?

40

I Don't Trust Anyone

> "God was in Christ reconciling the world to Himself, not counting their wrongdoings against them" (2 Corinthians 5:19, NASB).

The young woman looked around at everyone in the courtroom with visible disdain. She was on the witness stand testifying about four years of sexual abuse from her biological father. He was seated next to his attorney, in handcuffs and shackles, listening to his daughter accuse him of terrible acts, but looking intently at his fingernails. She described in detail how he had used her as a sexual object from the age of twelve until she turned sixteen. When she was eleven, Child Protective Services had taken away her mother's parental rights. Her mother had burned the soles of her feet because she didn't come back to the house on time. That's when she fell into her father's hands, who didn't wait long to use and abuse her. He intimidated her to keep the secret with a mix of gifts and threats. After the district attorney finished the direct questioning of the girl, the man's public defender began her own interrogatory.

"Young lady, if all you've alleged is true, why didn't you say anything to your aunt, doctor, your grandmother, a teacher at school, or someone you trust?"

Without hesitating, the teen replied, "It's because I don't trust anybody. Everyone who was supposed to care for me has betrayed me. That's why I didn't open my mouth, because I can't trust anybody! Let everyone rot in hell, starting with that damned man who called himself my father, who tore up my life!" Her tears, sighs, and sobs came from pain, but her expletives were open fury.

Psychologists affirm that beginning at birth, the first feeling developed in infancy is trust. According to psychologist Erik Erikson, trust is crucial for developing satisfying relationships throughout life. Trust is developed beginning at birth and through the first eighteen months. If instead, the child develops mistrust, there's a high possibility of that child progressing into juvenile and adult criminal behavior. Trust is developed with simple infant/adult interactions. The child cries, and the parent feeds it or changes its diaper. When the child's needs are met, trust begins to develop. Otherwise, the child develops anger, resentment, and a feeling of persisting abandonment. This mistrust is a potential feeder emotion for later violence, depression, drug and alcohol abuse, and other addictions.

A person's capacity to believe in a loving God is also radically diminished. The person only believes in the constant pain and hurt caused by the memories of neglect and abuse. When confronted by the claim that a loving God exists, immediately they ask, "Well, if that is so, why did that God allow all the pain and abuse to happen to me?" But God doesn't answer the question, at least the way we would like. God just shows us the life of his Son, Jesus the Christ. His entire being was abused beyond imagination. But many who have suffered abuse at the hands of their parents will immediately claim that all abuse began precisely with the story of Christ's suffering, that God himself condones abuse. Without putting ourselves in the abused victim's broken soul, we cannot blame anyone for thinking this.

But the truth is another. In Christ, God took upon himself all the pain and abuse sinful humanity has inflicted upon itself. The error of viewing God as a Father inflicting abuse upon the Son arises from a misconception about Jesus. This idea views Jesus as altogether human. But we must remember that Scripture affirms that Jesus was also fully divine. His humanity was fully united with his divinity. "In the beginning was the Word, and the Word was with God, and the Word was God. He was with God in the beginning" (John 1:1-2, NIV). Or as the Creed states, "very God of very God . . . being of one substance with the Father." Only if we separate the human Christ from the divine Christ would there be a basis for the allegation of "divine child abuse" as condoning human violence and abuse. But

"God was in Christ reconciling the world to Himself, not counting their wrongdoings against them" (2 Corinthians 5:19, NASB). The work of the cross was a Trinitarian joint and *voluntary* operation. The Father, the Son, and the Holy Spirit were on the cross taking away the sin of the world. When the prophet prophesied the work of the Messiah, he was including the entire divinity.

> Surely he took up our pain and bore our suffering, yet we considered him punished by God, stricken by him, and afflicted. But he was pierced for our transgressions, he was crushed for our iniquities; the punishment that brought us peace was on him, and by his wounds we are healed. We all, like sheep, have gone astray, each of us has turned to our own way; and the Lord has laid on him the iniquity of us all (Isaiah 53:4-6, NIV).

Notice that the prophet even foretold our misunderstanding of Christ's work: "we considered him punished by God" (v. 4). But it was the triune God on the cross, lifting from humanity all its sin, violence, and abuse, the half of which has not been told.

That is why we can trust again. Because at the cross, all the pain inflicted on us – merited or unmerited – was absorbed, taken up, assimilated, and taken away by God in the person of Christ who voluntarily received it all. Today, we can take our pain and leave it where it already is: in the God who wipes our tears away. Breathe deep and let it go. You are free to trust and love again, and forever!

41

Don't You Know My Own Story?

> "We love him because he loved us first (1 John 4:19, NLV). "'He himself bore our sins' in his body on the cross, so that we might die to sins and live for righteousness; 'by his wounds you have been healed'" (1 Peter 2:24, NIV).

"You should understand that the girl you are adopting is the daughter of a drug addict. The mother was using cocaine all through her pregnancy. Finally, someone reported her to the Child Protection Services. When the baby was born, we immediately took over her care. Today, five years later, the mother is still serving time at the penitentiary for that and other crimes for which she was convicted."

It was an adoption hearing, and the director of the program was discharging her duty to inform the adoptive parents about Lupita's past. She was a beautiful girl with huge black eyes and a satin chocolate complexion. Her hair fell in two carefully arranged braids on her shoulders, and she was coloring at a certain distance in the courtroom. The adoptive parents listened attentively. The director continued. "You should know that according to the statistics, beginning in her teen years, the girl will seek out drugs, for she was born with a tendency for cocaine. In fact, she was positive for cocaine at birth. She may also suffer other mental deficiencies and psychological trauma. Knowing all this, do you still want to adopt Lupita?"

"Lady," answered the prospective mother. "Don't you know my own story?"

"No," responded the director.

The mother continued, “I’ll make it as short as I can. I’m also a drug addict’s daughter. I was also given away in adoption. I would not be alive today but for the love of my adoptive parents. Their love saved my life. We want to do the same for Lupita.” When she heard her name, the girl came running. She jumped up on her adoptive mother’s lap, hung her arms around her neck, kissed and hugged her until she nestled quietly in her lap. They had been her foster parents almost since birth, and were now legally adopting her.

I overheard the program director whisper to herself, “That girl is going to beat all the odds.”

When Jesus was born in Bethlehem’s manger, he was not only creating a beautiful story that would be told year after year. The child Jesus was also taking on himself the history of the entire human race. Beginning at Mary’s lap, Jesus’s history would be yours and mine. Due to his love for us, in his flesh he drew us into him. That bitter cup that he would later drink to its dregs contained all the history of humanity at its worst, with all its hate and wars. Our own personal history was there as well; our worst and ugliest moments were there. He did not die for our best moments, but for our darkest secrets—all that we would never want anyone to know about ourselves.

The sufferings of Christ went beyond the pain of the nails in his hands and feet, greater than the insufferable crown of thorns on his head, more than the slow asphyxiation as he hung on the cross. No. His suffering content was our own history. He suffered all the agony and pain that we’ve ever experienced in our own lives.

What have you been addicted to? How have you been causing pain to yourself? What guilt do you carry in your heart? There’s nothing in your history that Christ did not already carry on the cross for you. That is why he loves and forgives us, because he knows our history, as the parents of the girl in our story knew her story. And the mother loved her because she had herself been rescued by the love of her adoptive parents. Scripture says, “We love because he first loved us” (1 John 4:19, NLV). Also, “‘He himself bore our sins’ in his body on the cross, so that we might die to sins and live for righteousness; ‘by his wounds you have been healed’” (1 Peter 2:24, NIV). That love was poured out for you and me. Don’t worry, cast away all fear. In Christ, we’ve already beaten all the odds.

42

He Is Not Your Son

> "Unto us a Son is given," "And you shall call his name Jesus, for he will save his people from their sins" (Isaiah 9:6, ASV; Matthew 1:21, ESV). "He who believes in him will not be disappointed" (1 Peter 2:6).

Their romance was soap opera material. She had been the poor girl in a faraway, neglected town, overworked and overprotected by her parents. But Prince Charming had come along and taken her to the land of promise. Soon she gave birth to a baby girl, although he wanted a boy. The years gave them certain prosperity, but at the cost of years of hardship and long hours of work. He held down a job as a bodyguard, chauffer, and errand boy for the top brass of a large company. She went to night school and was able to complete a high school education. A few years later, she was pregnant again, but once again . . . another girl. The father's hopes for a boy were dashed one more time. Their hard work and the upkeep of the house stressed the relationship of the once loving couple. A few more years went by. He worked at the same company; she continued her education until she landed a job as an administrative assistant in a large corporation. Then suddenly, pregnant again! She hid the news until getting the sonogram. Picture in hand, she surprised her husband: "At last, you're going to have the boy you wanted!" Energized by the news, they prepared the boy's room. The husband could hardly contain his joy. He shared the news with everyone, cigars and all! They both got respective baby showers. Finally, the boy was born, and duly given the dad's name.

There was happiness, laughter, and the high hopes of what that boy meant to them. But the mother could no longer play pretend. Her conscience would not leave her alone. Soon she was depressed: tears, sadness, irritability, and melancholy. One day, she could no longer hold it back. With tears in her eyes, she confessed to her husband, "I'm so sorry, love, but that is not your son." Now they were in Family Law Court finalizing their divorce.

"Unto us a Son is given," was the prophet's announcement. The angel later confirmed it to Mary: "And you shall call his name Jesus, for he will save his people from their sins" (Isaiah 9:6, ASV; Matthew 1:21, ESV). This boy was so awaited by the prophets that one of them called him "the desire of all nations" (Haggai 2:7, KJ21). Abraham was overjoyed because he was permitted to see in a vision the day when the Christ gave himself as the Lamb of God sacrificed for his sins (John 8:56). The Virgin Mary received the surprise announcement: "The Holy Spirit will come on you, and the power of the Most High will overshadow you. Therefore also the holy one who is born from you will be called the Son of God" (Luke 1:35, LEB). This son is given unto us, is ours, and forever. Scripture affirms, "Behold, I lay in Zion a chief cornerstone, chosen and precious: He who believes in him will not be disappointed" (1 Peter 2:6, WEB). It's impossible for us to imagine the disappointment, the shame, the anger and fury felt by the father of our story when his wife confessed to him that the boy was not his son. His hopes were certainly dashed into pieces, which could not be put together again. It is not so with our Son. The prophet affirmed, "Unto us a son is given." There is no deceit in those words. We already have the Desire of our hearts. We already have our awaited redemption, obtained by our Son, given by God's grace to all humanity. Abraham saw it as a future event. But we can see it by looking at the cross as the central historic marker, a *fait accompli* – a done deal – in our favor. In Christ the Son, we have forgiveness of all our sins, and eternal life at his side.

43
You Knew What You Were Doing

> "Have this mind among yourselves, which is yours in Christ Jesus, who, though he was in the form of God, did not count equality with God a thing to be grasped, but emptied himself, taking the form of a servant, being born in the likeness of men. And being found in human form he humbled himself and became obedient unto death, even death on a cross" (Philippians 2:5-8, ESV).

It was Christmas day in the capital of a Latin American country, and the mother could not find her five-year-old daughter. The girl and her dad seemed to have disappeared. As they had agreed, the mother let her daughter go and spend the 23rd and Christmas Eve with her dad. Then he was to bring her back and spend Christmas day with her mother. She looked for her little girl along the park where they would often go for walks. Anxiety crawled all over her body. With a racing heartbeat, she came back home to check her email once more. There she read the startling news: "Neyla and I arrived safely in New York. Merry Christmas."

The scream originated at the bottom of her gut and exploded through her throat. "How did it happen? He took her; he took her! And I didn't even suspect it! My daughter! How did he take her out of the country?" The father had threatened to do just that on several occasions. Now it was a cruel reality. The mother spent all she had in contacting the immigration authorities in her own country, the

American embassy, and then in traveling to the United States where she filed suit against him.

Hoping to evade the law, the father had moved to the west coast, but could not evade federal intelligence. He was being tracked by federal agencies, and finally brought to answer charges in a local court. The Family Law judge was severe. "You planned everything carefully and methodically. You falsified the mother's signature to get your daughter out of the country. You paid off the local authorities. You knew what you were doing. This was no casual father-daughter trip. Neyla will return to her home country with her mother."

Now it was the father's turn to scream, but he was drowned out by the mother's cry of joy. He was arrested immediately by federal agents present in court and charged with the kidnapping of a minor, international human trafficking, forging passports, and illegal transport of a minor as an act of international terrorism. The reunion of mother and daughter in the courtroom was moving beyond description, as both hugged and cried in each other's arms.

In the person of Jesus Christ, heaven emptied itself to rescue us. We are God's beloved children. Our age doesn't matter; to him, we are all like that five-year-old girl. Vulnerable to deceit, helpless to resist, needing much affection, tender care, protection, and above all, a joyful home. But an enemy deceived us and pretended to be our God. He counterfeits God's love with imitation affection, enchanting promises, and what appear to be miracles so that we will take casual walks with him, and eventually be trapped in his snares. But God's love is immensely passionate and jealous. He tracked us down. He saw us kidnapped and in the hands of a traitor. Scripture says that in Christ, all heaven was given to judge the enemy and free us from our captor. "Have this mind among yourselves, which is yours in Christ Jesus, who, though he was in the form of God, did not count equality with God a thing to be grasped, but emptied himself, taking the form of a servant, being born in the likeness of men. And being found in human form he humbled himself and became obedient unto death, even death on a cross" (Philippians 2:5-8, ESV). This was how God "has rescued us from the dominion of darkness and brought us into the kingdom of the Son he loves, in whom we have redemption, the forgiveness of sins" (Colossians 1:13-14, NIV). There's no better news than the Judge's verdict, "I will come again and take you to be with me, so that you may also be where I am. Do not let your heart be troubled, and do not let it be afraid" (John 14:3, 27, EHV). Even now we can hug and cry with joy as we throw our arms around our heavenly Father for such a great salvation!

44

I Refuse To Pay; He's Not My Son!

> "He made from one blood all nations who live on the earth . . . It is in Him that we live and move and keep on living" (Acts 17:26, 28, NLV).

The young woman was appearing before the Family Law judge, was petitioning that her ex-boyfriend, who was behind in his child support payments, pay in full and continue making monthly payments. She claimed that he had only been paying for the oldest child, a five-year-old boy, but wasn't paying for Eddy, now fourteen months old. The couple had separated some six months back. The mother, quite indignantly insisted, "Your Honor, he's disobeying the very orders you gave him six months ago. He hasn't paid once cent for the boy, and Eddy is still in diapers!"

"Well then," said the judge addressing the young man. "What do you have to say about all this, young man?"

"Well, Your Honor, "before anything else, I have a $500.00 bill here for Karen to pay."

"What?" interrupted the young mother. "A bill for what? I'm not going to pay for anything!" she responded, quite upset.

"What's your bill all about, young man?" asked the judge.

"If you remember, Your Honor, when we were here last time about six months ago, and you gave the child support order, I requested a DNA test to see if the child was mine. We agreed to this: If the child were mine, I would pay for the test. If the child were not mine, she would pay for it. Here's the bill, and she needs to pay for it."

"That's a lie, Your Honor," she cried out.

"Young man, please hand me the envelope with the results." The judge looked over the lab report, and then read out loud: "There's a 99.99 percent probability that this young man is *not* Eddy's father."

"Don't believe it, Your Honor. It's fake! That can't be true! Tell him to pay what he owes!" she exclaimed indignantly.

"But Your Honor," answered the man, "I refuse to pay! How am I going to pay for a child that doesn't carry my blood?"

The judge resolved the matter by calling the lab. He verified the test numbers, and confirmed the validity of the results. "Madam, the young man is within his rights. I'm sure there's another father somewhere out there that should appear in answer to your claim. But this man here does not have to pay. I order you to pay for the test as agreed before."

Scripture affirms that God "has made from one blood every nation" (Acts 17:26, NLV). Here the Greek word for "nation" is *ethnos,* from which our word "ethnic" comes. It refers to groups of people bound together by similar cultures and languages, the world over. But the text also says that from "one blood," God has made every single individual that has ever lived or will live. That is the blood from the one-man Adam, our first father. With a small "f." He failed us. God had breathed into him "the breath of life," yet he bequeathed to us the breath of death. Further, his blood, which could have given all humanity life, lost its life-giving power. He had been given an assignment, the father of the race. But he was fooled into wanting something greater, "the god of the race." He had believed the deceiver's lie: "For God [Elohim] knows that in the day you eat from it, your eyes will be opened, and you will be like God [Elohim], knowing good and evil." (Genesis 3:5, LSB). So, in desiring a promotion to "godhood," he lost our "fatherhood." As a result, his tenure as our father was transitory. Yet it had grave consequences for us. It brought us physical and spiritual death, poverty, injustice, pain, suffering, hatred, war, ecological ruin, and every kind of evil and curse that has ever entered into the human imagination.

Adam was totally unable to undo what he had done. He went bankrupt from the start and had no inheritance to leave us except evil.

And God saw what had been done, and it was not good. So God set into motion something already done: "The Lamb slain from the foundation of the world" (Revelation 13:7, PHILLIPS). And behold, all of Christ's work of salvation was very good.

Of all this, the prophet wrote: "For to us a child is born, to us a son is given, and the government will be on his shoulders. And he will be called Wonderful Counselor, Mighty God, Everlasting Father, Prince of Peace" (Isaiah 9:6, NIV). Did you see it? "Everlasting Father." The Messiah, the Christ himself, is our Father, who became flesh, lived among us, did not believe the tempter's lies, lived and loved according to the will of God, breathed on us the breath of life, and in his blood gave us eternal life-giving blood. For "the life of the body is in the blood . . . [Because] It is the blood that removes the sins, because it is life" (Leviticus 17:11, EXB). "Then he took a cup, and when he had given thanks, he gave it to them, saying, 'Drink from it, all of you. This is my blood of the covenant, which is poured out for many for the forgiveness of sins'" (Matthew 26-27, NIV).

"See what great love the Father has lavished on us, that we should be called children of God! And that is what we are! The reason the world does not know us is that it did not know him. Dear friends, now we are children of God, and what we will be has not yet been made known. But we know that when Christ appears,[a] we shall be like him, for we shall see him as he is" (1 John 3:1-2, NIV).

In giving us his spiritual life, Christ can only affirm that we have his DNA!

45

I Didn't Yell!

> "Then I saw another angel flying high overhead, with everlasting good news to announce to those who dwell on earth . . . Worship him who made" (Revelation 14:6, 7, NABRE).

Two women, each about forty-five years old came before the judge. Each had filed a restraining order against the other. They were neighbors, and even cousins! Each had daughters about the same age, in their mid-teens, studying at the same school. Each of the mothers left their homes about the same time of the morning headed in the same direction. But as they approached the entrance to the school, according to the Plaintiff, the other would cut in front of her, almost causing accidents in the school zone. They would lower the windows in their cars and yell insults at each other and their nieces, with hand gestures to punctuate their insults. As the Plaintiff presented her allegations, her tone was deliberate, calm, in control of herself. After listening to her, the judge requested the other cousin, the Defendant, to respond to the allegations.

"Your Honor," she began, also deliberately and composed. But as she recounted the same incidents, her volume increased until she was speaking at the top of her voice, "I DID NOT YELL AT THAT WOMAN!" At the end it was a full-blown scream so when she stopped, the last syllables echoed in the chamber.

As I translated her words, I looked at the judge and saw a faint smile at the corners of his mouth. His eyes were bright with mischief because (as he later told me) his strategy had been to let each woman go on until one of them accused herself with the tone of her voice. The judge did not hesitate to rule in favor of the Plaintiff. When the judge explained to her that her scream had exposed her, she denied it with another high volume, "I DID NOT YELL AT HER JUST NOW!" Everyone in the audience laughed out loud at the irony of the moment. Then the judge continued, "Everything here is recorded. Would you like to hear the recording?" Indignantly, the woman took her purse, and with a dramatic flair, strutted out of the courtroom.

The day will come when all the inhabitants of the earth, the living and the dead, will appear before the judgment seat of God. Jesus described the scene and predicted what would happen. "Not everyone who says to me, 'Lord, Lord,' will enter the kingdom of heaven, but only the one who does the will of my Father in heaven. Many will say to me on that day, 'Lord, Lord, did we not prophesy in your name? Did we not drive out demons in your name? Did we not do mighty deeds in your name?' Then I will declare to them solemnly, 'I never knew you. Depart from me, you evildoers'" (Matthew 7:21-23, NABRE). In other words, "Those who strut around their good works are shouting out loud that they haven't done any, because if they had done something in my name, I would have heard it, and paid attention. All they did was nothing but song and dance to make themselves look righteous and religious when they were nothing but doers of every kind of evil mischief." The irony is that the Christ has a name for all their prophesying, demon casting, and mighty deeding: evildoing. Their self-interest gives them away. Their high-pitched screams denouncing evil are only intended to cover their hatred, lust, anger, and other multiple vices. Yet, while they denounce their neighbor for such vices, they are raking in the profits from their fake deeds! No wonder the Lord calls all that evildoing.

But there is a voice that drowns out such trumpeting. Scripture describes it: "Then I saw another angel flying high overhead, with everlasting good news to announce to those who dwell on earth, to every nation, tribe, tongue, and people. He said in a loud voice, "Fear God and give him glory, for his time has come to sit in judgment. Worship him who made heaven and earth and sea and springs of water" (Revelation 14:6-7, NABRE). The end of the old and the beginning of the new is so great and glorious that the angel proclaims it at the top of its voice: "All creation, all nations, tongues, and peoples have been reconciled in Christ." The Gospel proclaims God's triumph in bringing back all things to himself. How his judgments come to an end is astounding. All nations will worship him with a great, united voice. And our voice is already recorded there. By faith we can hear it just now.

46

The Rehab Graduate

> "Then Jesus answered her, 'O woman, great is your faith! Be it done for you as you desire . . . "For the Son of Man came to seek and to save the lost" (Matthew 15:28, Luke 19:10, ESV).

It was the last session of the drug rehab program. The judge was the first to speak. "Today, as you graduate from this program, *you* are the evidence of our program's success. The court's intention was not to punish you for drug use, but to rehabilitate you, to give back to you what the drugs took from you, and more. During these last twelve months, you have not missed the therapies; you've turned in all your assignments, and have tested clean in all your drug tests. Further, today all pending charges against you are exonerated; your record is deemed clean. It's as if you had never committed the crime charged against you. In fact, as you submit job applications in the job market, you can even state that you were never arrested for this violation of the Health and Safety Code. Due to your successful participation in the program, you are deemed as having a clean record. It's as if you had no criminal history. I invite all present to congratulate all of you with a big applause." Due applause was given; the graduates received their diplomas and left the courtroom with a happy murmur of joyful chatter.

In the hallway, I recognized a participant for whom I had translated before and congratulated her. She quickly responded, "Ha, ha. Truth is, I didn't get caught. In the program I learned to say what they wanted to hear; I only used stuff with a short hit. In other words, I did what I needed to do to get them off my back. Ha, ha. What do you think?"

Shocked by her candor, I didn't know quite what to say. "Then I don't know whether to congratulate you or to wish you don't have to go through this again, or worse. But I see you are all dressed up with your friends; are you going to celebrate?"

"Well, but of course," she answered coyly. Then patting her purse, she added, "and here I have all we need. Tonight, we party at my apartment. Do you wanna come over? You're invited!"

Law and program-based rehabilitation programs may justify a wrongdoer before the laws of the land, but they do nothing to justify anyone before God. Our program's young woman graduate is a prime example. She had her certificate of rehabilitation; she had learned to give all the perfect answers, work all the steps, but her biggest pride was that she "didn't get caught." Her performance of the law did nothing to cut her cravings for drugs and the lifestyle that went with it. With law-based programs, she is caught in a never-ending spiral, perhaps to bounce from one program to another, until either her body or mind breaks down, hitting rock bottom with nowhere to go.

There's much preaching today that offers law-based "spiritual transformation" programs, although it doesn't sound law based. It has all the sounds and looks of something God would like to see. More prayer, more mind control of evil thoughts, more surrender to God, more pleading for the indwelling of God's Spirit so that the sinner may have more and more strength to resist temptation, and a greater use of our willpower. More worship, more lifting of the hands, more enraptured experiences, more spiritually uplifting emotions, and more testifying of our change from our old life to our new life. And yet, at the end, no matter how sincere (or hypocritical) the participation, we are no better off than the girl of our story. Our heart still wants to party. And with a partying heart, God grants no graduation certificate. Because "The Lord sees not as man sees; man looks on the outward appearance, but the Lord looks on the heart" (1 Samuel 16:7, ESV).

There's no doubt God's desire is for us to live cleaner, trouble-free lives. We should eagerly desire the same. Our families really want it. Society craves for such people. But – and this is Scripture's huge "but" – "No one will be declared righteous in God's sight by works of the law, for through the law we become aware of sin" (Romans 3:20). And for those who do not become aware of sin, the law has another more nefarious consequence: It stirs up their desire to sin until they do! This is true for everyone, believer or unbeliever, including great preachers of the Word, such as the apostle Paul. He clearly confessed,

> I did not know sin except through the law, and I did not know what it is to covet except that the law said, "You shall not covet." But sin, finding an opportunity in the commandment, produced in me every kind of covetousness. Apart from the law sin is dead. I once lived outside the law, but when the commandment came, sin became alive; then I died, and the commandment that was for life turned out to be death for me. For sin, seizing an opportunity in the commandment, deceived me and through it put me to death (Romans 7:7-11, NABRE).

Incredible! "Apart from the law sin is dead; when the commandment came, sin became alive; sin seized an opportunity in the commandment." Paul was not done: sin became "sinful" beyond measure through the commandment (v. 13). Sounds like the graduate of our story. The rehab program based on laws and regulations only awakened in her the desire to cheat, deceive, do more drugs, and involve other "graduates" in the same degradation! That's why through the works of the law, no one can be declared righteous before God. Divine law will never be satisfied with mere performance and apparent achievements. The law will always exclaim, "But you also have to provide a clean heart, but there's more honesty you can give, and so on. The "buts" of the law are endless.

However, the Scriptures at this point counter the law's "but" with a more powerful *but:*

"But now, completely apart from the law, a righteousness from God has been made known. The Law and the Prophets testify to it. This righteousness from God comes through faith in Jesus Christ to all and over all who believe (Romans 3:21-22, EHV).

Substitute "completed program" with "righteousness from God." God gave his Son, Jesus, the most difficult assignment: To complete the righteousness program for all human beings, so that they may be forgiven and declared righteous (justified). How? By believing it is true! "Through faith in Jesus Christ." That is even more incredible! That is good news for all who have hit rock bottom and in despair realize there is no way out through any law program. By faith alone in the completed program of Christ, they are program graduates and accepted into God's society forever, as if they had never sinned. Christ took both the penalty of their sin and completed the program on their behalf. Then he invites us not to party a là style of the law, but to feast in the greatest feast of all time: A wedding feast between him and all program graduates, who will not bring their own goods to the feast. Christ himself will provide the bread and the wine, sustainers and givers of his life forever! Do you want to come over? You're invited!

47

Can't I Have Just A Little Sip?

> "My Father, if it is possible, let this cup pass from me. Yet not as I will, but as you will" (Matthew 26:39, EHV).

Child Custody court grants parents certain periods of time to reunite with their children. This is because the Child Protection Agency removes them from the parents' custody. Most often, it is due to child abuse, negligence, or drug and alcohol abuse by the parents. During the allotted periods of time, the parents wishing to reunite with their children must participate in rehabilitation programs. There are drug rehab programs, alcohol recovery, parenting classes, and anger management. Parents must also have supervised visits with their children, generally in a foster home. On this particular occasion, a twenty-seven-year-old mother appeared before the court. Today the judge would review her participation in various programs and decide if she had met the requirements, or if she would lose all parenting rights over her three young children. They had gone from one foster home to another, awaiting their mother's recovery. The father's whereabouts were unknown. But the mother's report was not too flattering. Three months before, the mother had run away from a rehabilitation facility, but went back repentant a few days later. They gave her drug tests, but she gave a dirty test. The judge struggled to find a legal way to give her another opportunity. The children's defense attorney opposed the judge's efforts. He claimed the mother did not deserve the additional recovery time, and if given the chance, would abuse the children again. Finally, the judge gave her a sober warning. "Lady, you've already had eighteen months for your recovery, but I'm thinking of giving you another six-month extension. But I must warn you. You must promise not to drink any alcohol at all during this time. Absolutely nothing.

The woman immediately asked if she could address the court. "Yes, you may, madam. What is it you want to say?"

"Your Honor, you mean to say that during these six months, I can't even have a little sip?"

The judge almost lost it. "Madam, after that request, I am revoking your parental rights over your three children. The children will be turned over for adoption." The mother's tears and cry of desperation availed her nothing. The judge ordered the bailiffs to remove her from the courtroom.

On a certain occasion, Jesus was arriving at Jerusalem along the surrounding hillsides of the great and populous city. Fixing his eyes upon the multitudes in the city feverishly seeking pleasure and earthly goods, their freedom and independence, Jesus's eyes filled with tears, and he exclaimed, "Jerusalem, Jerusalem . . . I have often wanted to gather your people, as a hen gathers her chicks under her wings. But you wouldn't let me" (Matthew 23:37, CEV).

But let's not think we are much better than the people of that city. Let's not think that we have wanted to take shelter under his wings. Instead, we have sought the false wings of our vices, our obsessions, greed, jealousies, hatreds, and struggles for power over others. We want one more sip of revenge against someone we think has harmed us, one last little white lie, one more little sip of our anger or lust. But still, he claims us as his own. "Can a woman forget her nursing child, fail to pity the child of her womb? Even these may forget, but I won't forget you" (Isaiah 49:15, CEB). That is why he does not tire of calling us, "Come to me, all you who are struggling hard and carrying heavy loads, and I will give you rest. Put on my yoke, and learn from me. I'm gentle and humble. And you will find rest for yourselves. My yoke is easy to bear, and my burden is light" (Matthew 11:28-30, CEB). The burden we carry is our out-of-control desire for those little sips. But some are also burdened by the weight of our good works, for they tempt us to think we are something. It weighs us down to think that for us to be sure that God accepts us, we need to offer him more and greater sacrifices, penitence, or perhaps to grovel and hate ourselves or our sins more and more! These are all little sips of selfishness, hypocrisy, and appearances. But all our little sips – be they of sin or apparent good works – make us drunk with a false sense of who we are. What's worse is that all there is in the cups we drink do nothing for us except condemn us. At the end, we down the cup of our condemnation one little sip at a time.

But Christ came just in time and snatched those cups from our hands, just before we would hurt ourselves with their eternal consequences.

In Gethsemane, he took the cups from our lips; he poured it into his own and drank the bitterness of our sins, to the last drop. There has been no sin, committed by any human being ever, that he did not drink and admitted into his holy being. And he did it to destroy its fateful venom. "My Father, if it is possible, let this cup pass from me. Yet not as I will, but as you will" (Matthew 26:39, EHV).

No, it wasn't us. Neither are we required to do it. It was Jesus who downed sip by sip the entire bitter cup of our sins. Our burden is to drink jarfuls of his plentiful forgiveness!

48

I Don't Have To Be A Criminal To Do Bad Things

> "Come now, and let us reason together, says the LORD. Though your sins are like scarlet, they will be as white as snow. Though they are as red as crimson, they will be like wool" (Isaiah 1:18, EHV).

"It's that the motorcycle stopped all of a sudden in front of me before I realized it."

"Sir, but your blood alcohol level tested at .14, six points over the .08 legal limit," answered the defense attorney.

"But I wasn't drunk; I had all five senses with me, nothing happened. It was just a little bump on the rear fender of the motorbike, that's all," retorted the defendant.

"Precisely," said the attorney. "That's the problem with drinking and driving. The driver does not realize that he has lost just a bit of reaction time, and you proved it. You think that the motorcycle stopped suddenly. But no, the bike just came to a normal stop at the traffic light. But the alcohol in your brain delayed your reaction time. That's why you hit it from the back. And it wasn't just a slight bump. Bike, driver, and the lady riding in the back all hit the ground."

"But nothing really happened to them; they got up just fine and wiped the dust," argued the defendant.

"Look," responded the attorney, now somewhat miffed. "I'm an amateur bicyclist. I go out and train on all these routes, including the one in which you hit the motorcycle. You know what scares me the most when I train? People like you who believe they do nothing wrong, who are basically good people. But you scare me, because good people like you could get me killed. What do you think would have happened if instead of bumping that large motorcycle you had hit my lightweight bicycle with me on it? You would have killed me or broken my neck!"

The young man kept silent this time. Then finally he said, "You're right. You don't have to be a criminal to do bad things."

With those few words, the young man finally began his road to recovery. Scripture says, "The fear of the Lord is the beginning of wisdom" (Proverbs 9:10, NIV). How true. But that fear of the Lord comes because God himself teaches us to fear all the harm we can cause without being criminals. A criminal is one whose career is doing bad things for his own satisfaction. Most of us dedicate ourselves to doing what is good, but even so, we do bad things. Without realizing it, we offend our neighbor. We are unaware of our capacity to do harm to people around us. We think we just bumped them a little, and it really wasn't our intention to cause them harm. However, we think they owe us an apology instead of us apologizing to them. We think that perhaps the neighbor should have watched out for himself a bit more.

The psalmist exclaimed, "Who could possibly know all that he has done wrong? Forgive my hidden and unknown faults" (Psalm 19:12, VOICE). That request has only one answer: Look at Jesus crucified in your place. Because there on the cross, the Son of God took all the hidden sins hidden in our heart, as well as those that are not so hidden, and died for each one of them. It is extremely grave that an innocent person should die so that we may finally realize the immense capacity we carry to harm others. What makes it worse is that we justify ourselves and deny our potential for evil when sin by harming others. We brush it off as something minor; we really didn't mean it, instead of praying "and forgive us our trespasses." Like the young man rear-ending the motorcycle, we run over Christ while drunk in our sins and trespasses. But he took them on himself, and died for them in our place.

However, on the third day he rose from the dead to give us an eternal embrace of love, peace, and forgiveness, holding us to himself forever. In other words, our "punishment" is to be eternally loved, and much more than "just a bit." However much we reduce and exonerate our guilt, infinitely more he magnifies his love for us, and his forgiveness. "Come now, let us reason together, says the Lord: though your sins are like scarlet, they shall be as white as snow; though they are red like crimson, they shall become like wool" (Isaiah 1:18, EHV).

49

It's Not Me In The Picture, It's My Boyfriend

> "I delight greatly in the Lord; my soul rejoices in my God. For he has clothed me with garments of salvation and arrayed me in a robe of his righteousness, as a bridegroom adorns his head like a priest, and as a bride adorns herself with her jewels" (Isaiah 61:10, NIV).

"It's not me in the picture; it's my boyfriend," and with those words the young woman handed to the bailiff the picture taken by the traffic control camera. Most drivers are already aware of this system of detecting traffic violations. As the car approaches an intersection where the light is already red, the camera is triggered, and in some, there's even a phosphorescent flash that catches a picture of the driver, a close up of the license plate, and the date and hour of the infraction. Then, the traffic control agency sends a ticket by mail to the owner of the vehicle.

Today, the young woman appeared before the traffic court judge to answer for a red-light violation. The judge asked the bailiff for her own opinion, if the person in the picture was the person present in court. She answered quickly, "That's absolutely a negative, Your Honor. The person driving the vehicle is a man."

"Very well," said the judge. "Do we have the boyfriend here?"

"I am the boyfriend," answered a strong, low voice from the back of the courtroom. "I plead guilty. She is innocent. I was driving."

The judge smiled. "Neither of you is guilty. The young lady is not guilty, because she's not the one in the picture. You are not guilty because there's no charge against you . . . And by the way, when is the wedding?"

"It's today!" said the woman, almost too quickly and too loudly. "We'll do it today, since we don't have to pay the ticket; we can get married sooner rather than later!"

"That's true," said the judge. "Enjoy your pardon!"

In this brief encounter, we see a small glimpse of the Gospel, God's Good News in Jesus Christ. He responds for us as our groom and husband. He pleads guilty on our behalf. He takes our sentence on himself. In his own body, he suffers the consequence of our sins, whether large or small. The evidence is there, for there's a recording of every moment of our lives. Then he delights in our pardon throughout eternity. And that is what all believers do with their lives in Jesus Christ. We enjoy and delight in his forgiveness. That's how the prophet Isaiah responded thousands of years ago: "I delight greatly in the Lord; my soul rejoices in my God. For he has clothed me with garments of salvation and arrayed me in a robe of his righteousness, as a bridegroom adorns his head like a priest, and as a bride adorns herself with her jewels" (Isaiah 61:10, NIV).

But there's something else in humanity's Groom. He takes our guilt, but in his own person, he's entirely innocent and not guilty, as the boyfriend of our story. Scripture says of Christ, "Such a high priest truly meets our need—one who is holy, blameless, pure, set apart from sinners, exalted above the heavens" (Hebrews 7:26, NIV). Only someone entirely pure and innocent could love us with perfect love. In the purity of his love, there is no doubt, resentment, impatience, or fits of anger; there's only a tender regard and patient affection, which always tells us, "I have taken your place in everything. You are mine, mine forever." "So do not fear, for I am with you; do not be dismayed, for I am your God. I will strengthen you and help you; I will uphold you with my righteous right hand" (Isaiah 41:10, NIV). Because "there will be more rejoicing in heaven over one sinner who repents than over ninety-nine righteous persons who do not need to repent" (Luke 15:7, NIV). Enjoy the pardon!

50

Your Petition Has No Merit

> "But our citizenship is in heaven. We are eagerly waiting for a Savior from there, the Lord Jesus Christ. By the power that enables him to subject all things to himself, he will transform our humble bodies to be like his glorious body" (Philippians 3:20-21, EHV).

His sunburned face, strong muscular body, and large biceps could not hide his age. He was a day laborer who had worked all his life in the agricultural fields. The graying hair on his temples contrasted with his bronzed and somewhat wrinkled face, marked by years of working in the sun. "Your Honor, as instructed by my immigration attorney, I come to withdraw a guilty plea I entered on a misdemeanor twenty-two years ago."

"And why did you wait so long?" answered the judge.

"It's that I didn't know that a misdemeanor like shoplifting was going to affect my request for citizenship status twenty-two years later."

"Well, let me take a look at your petition . . . Here you state that no one read to you the immigration consequences when you plead guilty. But I'm looking right now at the computer transcript of that hearing. Here is a check mark beside this statement: 'I understand that by pleading guilty, I may be deported, denied legal entry to this country, as well as citizenship.' Do you remember placing a check mark beside that statement and signing below?"

"No, Your Honor. I don't remember anybody reading anything like that to me," answered the defendant.

"Well, let me give you a copy." With copy in hand, the judge addressed him once again, "Is that your signature on that plea form? Just above your signature it states, "I have read and understood this entire document."

After a short pause, the man responded, "That was twenty-two years ago, Your Honor. I don't remember anyone telling me anything like that."

To which the judge responded, "Next to your signature is the signature of the interpreter stating that she translated the entire document to you. There's no legal merit to your petition. It is denied."

That's how we appear before the judgment seat of God. We come with our noblest and purest intentions. We've worked all our lives serving others, and working for their best interest. But we too have our own interests. We'd like citizenship in God's Kingdom in exchange for the very best we can offer God. There are indeed many who, upon serious introspection, believe there's nothing in their life God would – or even could – reject. They've never been into any addiction, not even tried out anything that could be abused. Their character is blameless. No one has anything bad to say about them; in fact, everyone has nothing but good things to say about them. They never lose their temper at anything; they have a most optimistic outlook on life and believe the best in others. In fact, they bring out the best in others. They never use bad words; no vulgarity crosses their lips when they pinch their fingers, just an honest "ouch." They feel rather offended at the Scriptural affirmation: "for all have sinned, and don't quite hit the mark of the glory of God." They feel they are within the circle of the target that gives them top score every time.

But even the slightest thought or feeling of offense at being lumped in with "everybody out there who is into sinning," is a grave offense against God. Why? Because it takes away the overarching scope of the grace of God in Christ Jesus. It makes his sacrifice unnecessary, at least for a select group of individuals who in their minds are truly able to "make it" on their own. If the sacrifice of Christ was necessary for some, that's just fine. But "don't pin me down as one for whom Jesus had to carry sins. I'm really not aware that at any point in my life, I have really sinned before God. My conscience is clear." People with this spiritual mindset actually exist. They really don't understand how they could ever be labeled as "sinners." Sure, they could always have done something better, although they cannot imagine how, since with all sincerity they believe they hit the mark every time. They have a quizzical look on their face when you talk to them about the blood of Christ being shed for the forgiveness of their sins, and very discretely let you know they would rather change the subject. But when the topic of the suffering of the wicked, and their eternal destruction comes up, they think such punishment is rather well-deserved for the wickedness and disobedience of "such evil people."

But to those with this mindset, the prophet's question still applies, "How long shall your evil thoughts lodge within you?" (Jeremiah 4:14, MEV). That's got to hurt. But the truth sets one free. Paul faced the same thinking among his own people. They thought they were the pinnacles of perfection, especially when they compared themselves with those perverse Gentiles. "You, therefore, have no excuse, you who pass judgment on someone else, for at whatever point you judge another, you are condemning yourself, because you who pass judgment do the same things" (Romans 2:1, NIV). When those who consider themselves pure, pass judgment on those they see as wicked, they replay in their minds whatever wickedness they are judging. As they replay and review those acts, their sinful nature kicks in and they end up mentally participating in the wickedness they are condemning. They end up in the same cesspool they are condemning. Further, they end up there without any grace, mercy, or forgiveness for themselves and those they judge. "So when you, a mere human being, pass judgment on them and yet do the same things, do you think you will escape God's judgment? Or do you show contempt for the riches of his kindness, forbearance and patience, not realizing that God's kindness is intended to lead you to repentance?" (Romans 2:3-4, NIV).

This is amazing. Paul tells the self-righteous that God's mercy toward those they consider wicked is designed to lead *them*, the self-righteous, to repentance! Then he gives to both, the wicked and the wickedly self-righteous, the goods of the gospel. "But now apart from the law the righteousness of God has been made known, to which the Law and the Prophets testify. This righteousness is given through faith in Jesus Christ to all who believe. There is no difference between Jew and Gentile, for all have sinned and fall short of the glory of God, and all are justified freely by his grace through the redemption that came by Christ Jesus. God presented Christ as a sacrifice of atonement, through the shedding of his blood—to be received by faith" (Romans 3:21-25, NIV).

It is faith, and faith alone, that lifts all of us from our cesspools, the cesspools of sin, and the cesspool of self-righteousness. That faith has as its object the righteousness of Christ, by which all of us are freely justified by his grace. Our petition for wiping our guilty sentence has legal merit: The shed blood of Jesus Christ, our Lord. And it is granted unconditionally and forever!

51

Do You Think She'll Come And Take Your Place?

> "Have this in your mind, which was also in Christ Jesus, who, existing in the form of God, didn't consider equality with God a thing to be grasped, but emptied himself, taking the form of a servant, being made in the likeness of men. And being found in human form, he humbled himself, becoming obedient to the point of death, yes, the death of the cross" (Philippians 2:5-10, WEB).

The attorney's tone of voice was urgent. I translated the interview. "Look sir, this case has already gone on for months, with no resolution in sight. If I had some defense to offer the jury, I would tell you, 'Let's go to trial.' But so far, you haven't given me one piece of evidence, or one lead that I can use in your defense. What I have is this: The house was in your name. Someone snitched on you. The cops came; they searched the property and found the drugs, cash, and weapons. Five large boxes weighing 140 pounds filled with cocaine, marijuana, meth, $120,000 dollars in cash, seven 9mm guns, and two automatic rifles. I've got to have some defense for you having all that stash. If you wish to go to trial with all that evidence stacked against you, most likely you'll be condemned. You were the only person at home; the house is in your name. But today the district attorney is making you a very good offer. If you go on to trial and lose, you'll get twenty years. But if today, yes, today, you plead guilty, you'll only get three."

"But, defend me, madam attorney. There's proof the stuff wasn't mine."

"Oh, really?" answered the attorney with a bit of sarcasm in her voice, "like, what?"

The man shot back, "Look for Mrs. Nelly del Campo. She'll tell you everything."

"Really? What's she going to tell me?"

"That all that stuff wasn't mine, that it was hers."

"And where am I going to find her?"

"Oh, she's just on the other side of the border. She lives there with her husband and five children," he retorted.

"Well, sir, but do you really think she's going to leave them all back home and come here and take your place in prison for twenty years?"

Our entire human race is in the same situation. It's condemned, with no defense, due to its unbelief, hate, and rejection of our neighbor, greed, oppression, and so much more—until its attorney was born in Bethlehem's manger. And what an attorney he turned out to be! He took our case much further than would be expected of an attorney. For he defended us by taking our place. He did leave everything that was his, his loved ones, his home from eternity, to take our place in the prison of our condemnation. Scripture says,

> "Have this in your mind, which was also in Christ Jesus, who, existing in the form of God, didn't consider equality with God a thing to be grasped, but emptied himself, taking the form of a servant, being made in the likeness of men. And being found in human form, he humbled himself, becoming obedient to the point of death, yes, the death of the cross. Therefore God also highly exalted him, and gave to him the name which is above every name, that at the name of Jesus every knee should bow, of those in heaven, those on earth, and those under the earth, and that every tongue should confess that Jesus Christ is Lord, to the glory of God the Father" (Philippians 2:5-11).

There on the cross, he crossed the border; he found us just as we were to receive our eternal death sentence, and then took our place, bearing the complete load of humanity's guilt. That is why he came. He did leave everything, even life itself, to take our place . . . But the most difficult part for us is . . . to believe it! But when we do, what peace, what joy, what freedom! We live on this side of the border, where everything we breathe, every step we take, is within the infinite boundaries of God's love.

52

Don't Set Foot Inside That Church!

> "God was reconciling the world to himself through Christ, by not counting people's sins against them . . .God caused the one who didn't know sin to be sin for our sake so that through him we could become the righteousness of God" (2 Corinthians 5:19-21, CEB).

A profound silence was felt in the courtroom when the judge announced the next case to be heard. It was a mother requesting a restraining order against her son. The judge granted the petition, which prohibited the son from approaching within 100 meters of the mother, father, sisters, brothers, their places of residence and work, even the same church. "Don't you set foot inside that church," the judge admonished him. Then, addressing the mother he asked her, "For how long do you want the restraining order?"

"For as long as possible, Your Honor."

"Then, it will be for the following five years," ordered the judge. I translated for both mother and son. The mother was to my left, the son to my right. I could feel the tension. They didn't even glance at each other.

The judge asked the well built, twenty-five-year-old man if he had something to respond to the allegations of physical abuse on his parents and siblings. His biceps doubled mine, and he flexed all his arm muscles as he spoke. In a mocking, threatening, dry tone he responded, "This old hag is lying. Truth is, none of them goodie-goodies has ever loved me; they're the ones who abused me when I was little, now they're complaining?"

Since I was sitting right next to him, I could catch the stench of alcohol on his breath. "I didn't abuse anyone that night, or ever! It's all a fib!" he laughed perversely. "Bring the cop who they called that night; he can't say anyone got hit that night! I deny all those charges. I'm gonna defend myself! It's all a bunch of lies!"

But the judge granted the order. He could not approach his family within 100 meters. He was ordered to have no contact by telephone, social media, or third party. Don't show up at the same church; don't even set foot on the parking lot. It would seem strange for a judge to order him to stay away from a place where he could hear God's Word, at least the same church that he had attended as a boy. The young man looked defiantly at the judge, then at everyone in court. Then he slammed and swiped the documents on the table, and strutted insolently out of the courtroom.

It is stranger yet to think on the cross, and see the person hanging there taking on his body all the fury, resentments, and perversity of the young man in the courtroom, and then dying for his sins. Scripture says, "God caused the one who didn't know sin to be sin for our sake so that through him we could become the righteousness of God" (2 Corinthians 5:21, CEB). God looks at this hardened and defiant young man through Jesus Christ, God's perfect Son. That way, God sees what no one else is able to see: someone noble, respectful, tender, affectionate, loving to his parents, considerate, and making sacrifices for his family. That love calls him – and us – to repentance. God wants us to repent from thinking that we are worthless and that God himself rejects us. God tells us the truth about ourselves. We are loved with a love that will last forever. Does God order us not to set foot in church or to go to one in particular? God certainly does not want us to go to church or any place where we'll be told that God will reject us, or that we are abandoned on account of our sins. But wherever we are told that we belong to God's family and our sins have been forgiven through Christ, that's where we set foot and stay. Against that invitation, there is no restraining order! The only order that was truly ever obeyed was the command Jesus received from the Father: You will go and rescue the most worthless and useless sinner, and then bring him home. And at the cross when Jesus breathed his last, he said, "It is done." With those words, he ended the million meters approach zone between the Father and us, and we are embraced in his love forever!

53

Papa Bear Or The Cubs?

"You didn't choose me, but I chose you and appointed you so that you could go and produce fruit and so that your fruit could last. As a result, whatever you ask the Father in my name, he will give you" (John 15:16, CEB).

The defense attorney was interviewing a young mother. I was translating. He asked her, "Don't you remember? Three months ago, when you were here last, the judge warned you: 'Your boyfriend has to leave the house. He can't be there at any moment or for any reason. Otherwise, the children run a huge risk. He will probably harm them again. If he doesn't leave the house, you will lose your kids and they will be placed in a foster home.' Last time, we read the report. The children stated to the social worker that he injects drugs into his arms in front of them. Then he loses control, and he yells, threatens, and beats them." Then he warned her again of the consequences.

She thought about it for a few moments, a faint smile crept on her face, and then said, "Yes, but . . ."

"There are not buts," the lawyer cut her off. "The social worker's report this time says that they went to the house and investigated. They found his clothes on your bed. He had even left his dirty socks on the floor. It seems he took off running when he saw the social worker walking to the house. Then, when the worker interviewed the children, they stated that he's still living there, and they are still very afraid of him because he yells at them and throws things at them for them to be quiet."

But the mother insisted, "You wouldn't believe how much he has changed in the last few weeks. He's still going to the programs. They've tested him, and he gives clean tests. He's holding down a job. He helps me with the rent and brings the groceries. I can't make it alone without him. I don't have a work permit. It's been two weeks since he last hit the children, and since he last injected himself."

The attorney once again interrupted her. "Lady, just a moment. Who are you protecting here? Papa bear or the cubs?"

She responded meekly, "It's that I love him too much; I can't live without him." When she gave the same answer to the judge a few minutes later, the woman lost her cubs—her two daughters and the young boy. The children were immediately removed from her care. She kept the Alpha bear.

In Jesus's third temptation, "the devil brought him to a very high mountain and showed him all the kingdoms of the world and their glory. [The devil] said, 'I'll give you all these if you bow down and worship me'" (Matthew 4:8-9, CEB). But when Jesus looked at the great multitudes in all those kingdoms, he saw that not one among them would be forgiven, and given eternal life. For that to happen, Jesus would have to go to the cross, become the horror of sin itself, take the place of all human beings before God's righteous wrath against sin, suffer the cruelest humiliation, and death, without any guarantee that he would outlive the trial.

But it was that very reality that moved his faith to persevere. In that temptation, he saw us defenseless, at the mercy of a cruel and lying despot who would finally cast us into the black hole of eternal perdition. He saw us even more lost than those little cubs of our story living under the threats and beatings of a cruel, furious, drugged and drunken father. Jesus then, instead of bowing in worship to the devil, bowed before the Father who had sent him with the mission to become one with us, and through his death, give us eternal life—but at a great cost to himself: his death, and death on the cross. Instead of defending himself, or surrender in greed and fear before the devil, he chose to protect the cubs. "You didn't choose me, but I chose you" (John 15:16, CEB). That's what he told his disciples, our forebears in the faith. In the end, it's not us who choose him. We are his chosen. His special treasure. Just as the children of our story were helpless to choose what was best for them, whether to stay with mom or dad, that's how we are. That's why Jesus did not hesitate. He chose us so that he could love us yesterday, love us today, and love us tomorrow. He chose us, his special cubs.

54

Stop The Trial; I'll Take The Twenty Years!

"For the wages of sin is death, but the gift of God is eternal life in Christ Jesus our Lord . . . and all are justified freely by his grace through the redemption that came by Christ Jesus" (Romans 6:23; 3:24, NIV). "For the Son of Man did not come to destroy men's lives, but to save them" (Luke 9:56, NIV).

The coroner found the body propped against the wall. He had two large openings: one in the abdomen, another one in the chest. Both had been caused by a sawed-off shot gun, fired at point-blank. The first shot perforated the intestines. The second destroyed the lungs and the heart. The coroner explained to the jury that the victim briefly survived the first shot, but the second caused his instant death. There were two .22 shells nearby, and pellets everywhere. Years before the jury trial, at the time of the incident, the police had wanted to question the victim's roommate, but couldn't find him. Ten years later, thanks to the cooperation of international police agencies, they found the suspect living in a town near the other side of the border. He was extradited and was now facing a jury trial in a criminal court. He had insisted on his innocence as early as his arrest. According to him, he had fled fearing that a gang would use him as a scapegoat and blame him for the grisly murder. Now, the jury listened to all the evidence against him. The twelve jurors had already been selected, sworn, and installed. His life was in their hands. Seven women, five men. All were strangers, but as the judge had instructed, they could show neither sympathy nor bias toward the defendant. The district attorney was very meticulous, carefully exacting every possible piece of testimony from the witnesses. Suddenly, the young man whispered to me. "Tell my attorney to stop this trial. I'll take the twenty years prison time they were offering me. I don't trust this jury, and with this clever district attorney, I'm sure they will sentence me to life.

That's a perfect picture of us. We spend our lives declaring our innocence before God and our neighbor. We insist we don't do any harm to anyone. We just do the best we can. We do our best to help others out when we can. If indeed there's a life after death, most likely we'll get there because we haven't been that bad. We buy into our own little lie whispered by our deceitful heart until we hear: "For all have sinned and fall short of the glory of God . . . For the wages of sin is death . . . there is no one who does good, not even one" (Romans 3:23; 6:23; 3:12, NIV). That's when panic hits. Like the young man of our story, we cry out, "Stop the judgment; I'm going to get condemned for sure. I'm lost." But that's the best moment of our lives, for Jesus stands in our favor and cries out louder than us, "But the gift of God is eternal life in Christ Jesus . . . being justified freely by his grace, through the redemption that is in Christ Jesus" (Romans 6:23; 3:25, NIV). "For the Son of Man "did not come to destroy men's lives, but to save them" (Luke 9:56, NIV). "For God so loved the world, that he gave his only Son, that whoever believes in him should not perish, but have everlasting life" (John 3:16, ESV). The young man of our story was not allowed to make a deal with his guilt once his trial started. He tried a bit too late. He was sentenced to life in prison. But it was not so with us: On the cross, Jesus shifted judgment from us to himself in the middle of our trial. And he was condemned instead of us. When he pled guilty in our place, we were freed, and freed to be with him forever!

55

You Lost Custody, I've Got It All

> "Father, I have sinned against heaven and against you, I am no longer worthy to be called your son . . . As I live, declares the Lord God, I have no pleasure in the death of the wicked . . . For the Son of Man came to seek and save the lost" (Luke 15:21, NIV; Ezekiel 33:11; Luke 19:10, ESV).

Their phone conversations always ended up in shouting matches. When they talked in person, it was worse. "You know what you did six years ago. You went drinking with your girlfriends, drove drunk, crashed, and now you're paying the consequences. You got deported. That's why you can't see the girls. You abandoned them with your drinking. You just can't be a mom when you feel like it. Well, no, you can't. Then while you were on the other side of the border living it up, I asked for full custody of the girls. Now you don't even have the right to see them. So quit asking. You can't see them; I already told you. They won't even know who you are. And if you keep on bothering me for the same thing, I'm going to report you to immigration so they kick you back again to the other side like they did last time. Are you listening to me?"

"But Miguel, look, I bought some cute little dresses for them, and I want to take them to church."

"No, you look. Go ahead and clean your toilet with those rags," went the back and forth. The insults wouldn't stop.

"Miguel, last year I only saw them twice."

"Yes, and I regret both times. I have right here the Family Court papers giving me everything. Don't even show up in court; they'll pick you up right from there and deport you. Remember you never paid the fine on that drunk driving case, and they have an arrest warrant for you. So forget the girls. They're mine! They don't even ask for you anymore!"

The mother could not tolerate it any longer, so she decided to throw herself at the mercy of the family court judge. She appeared and requested at least partial custody. She showed the judge proof that she had completed all her DUI programs, paid her fines, was holding down a job, and had an adequate place to live with the girls. To her surprise, the judge told her the father had never filed a custody petition. He'd just been threatening her with a made-up story! The judge was not pleased at all with the father's strategy, and only gave him supervised visits. The mother was given full legal and physical custody.

That's how it is with us. When we come to God with a broken heart, hurt, and desperate for peace and forgiveness, the accuser shows up. "You've lost all your rights to come before God and ask forgiveness. Your sins are way too many, and too huge and disgusting. So go ahead, and you'll see how he'll reject and condemn you, because your case is hopeless; not even God can fix you!" That is Satan's work—to accuse us.

But Jesus's work and words are totally the opposite. He told the story of the son who went to a far-off land, and there wasted his father's inheritance on fun and games. At the end, he found himself eating the leftovers from the scraps thrown to the pigs! But he remembered his father's compassion. He must have struggled with doubt: "My dad will never forgive me; he'll turn me over to the authorities for wasting his money." But nothing could erase from his memory his father's loving and forgiving spirit. He'd chance it on his dad; he'd throw himself at his mercy. He prepared his little speech: "Father, I have sinned against heaven and against you, I am no longer worthy to be called your son" (Luke 15:21, NIV). But just as his father went out to meet him and didn't listen to his speech, so our heavenly Father cries out for us, "As surely as I live, declares the Sovereign Lord, I take no pleasure in the death of the wicked, but rather that they turn from their ways and live. Turn! Turn from your evil ways!" (Ezekiel 33:11, ESV). Don't listen to the voice of the accuser. Listen to the voice that forgave you from the cross: "I have come to seek and save that which had been lost" (Luke 19:10, ESV).

56

I Saw Those Feet Just Hanging There

> "But because of his great love for us, God, who is rich in mercy, made us alive with Christ even when we were dead in transgressions—it is by grace you have been saved. And God raised us up with Christ and seated us with him in the heavenly realms in Christ Jesus" (Ephesians 2:4-6, NIV).

"When we got there with the fire engine, there was smoke coming from the front windows, and flames from the rear windows. My team got ready to enter the residence. We found the front door locked and had to knock it down. The living room was engulfed in smoke. There was hardly any visibility. As I crawled along the floor, I saw those feet just hanging from the recliner. I gently and slowly pulled on them until the man fell to the carpet; crawling again, I pulled him to the front door and safety. He was unconscious. He had been overcome by smoke inhalation. His body was covered with ashes. In the apartment next door, a mother with her three children was still sleeping; they were also rescued. In just a few minutes, the fire was out. Someone had lit the fire in the kitchen and two of the bedrooms." It was the fire captain giving testimony before the jury. He continued, "When we investigated, it was the same man on the sofa who had lit the fire. He'd gotten drunk and lit the fire, intending to take his life. It seems he suffers from mental health problems because he's been drinking since he was a child. He almost succeeded in taking his life, and the life of the mother and her three children next door." The man was arrested as soon as he was released from the hospital. Now he was answering to charges of attempted homicide, arson, destruction of property not his own, and a few others. I was translating the hearing for the man. As I made eye contact with him, he motioned for me to approach him.

"Listen," he whispered. "Tell my attorney that I don't remember a thing!"

The man of our story had condemned himself to a sure death by lighting a fire inside his own house. A few more minutes and he, together with his neighbor and her three girls, would have succumbed to smoke and flames. But their rescuer arrived, and just in time. The fire captain didn't ask, "What kind of man is this? With all these empty beer cans on the floor, does he deserve to be rescued?"

No! The savior has only one thing in mind: To save! If that's the way it is with first responders, God's intention is more single minded yet. "But because of his great love for us, God, who is rich in mercy, made us alive with Christ even when we were dead in transgressions—it is by grace you have been saved. And God raised us up with Christ and seated us with him in the heavenly realms in Christ Jesus" (Ephesians 2:4-6, NIV). What? Did he die to save criminals and drunks? Yes. Specially to save them, because "It is not the healthy who need a doctor, but the sick. I have not come to call the righteous, but sinners" (Mark 2:17, NIV). Our illness also includes a bad memory, for we also say about our offenses against our neighbor, "I don't remember a thing!" That's how we justify ourselves, alleging we owe no one anything. But God, who in an instant could erase us from his memory, is the one that says, "I, even I, am he who blots out your transgressions, for my own sake, and remembers your sins no more" (Isaiah 43:25, NIV). If that were so, what would be your Rescuer's first words to you?

57

A Dad, Little By Little

> "We also have come to know and trust the love that God has for us. God is love. Whoever remains in love remains in God and God in him . . . We love because he first loved us" . . . "My cup is overflowing. Surely goodness and mercy will pursue me all the days of my life, and I will live in the house of the Lord forever" (1 John 14:16, 19; Psalm 23:5-6, EHV).

"But Madam Judge, this man abandoned me five years ago, with a two-year-old and a newborn. I've been a single mother all these years, and now he has the gall to come back saying he now wants to be a dad! It's not fair, Your Honor. Don't give him visits with the children. They don't even know who he is. It's as if they were going away with a stranger!" The sighs and laments of the mother filled the silence of the courtroom.

But the judge retorted, "Do you know what's *not* fair?"

"No, no I don't know," answered the mother amidst her tears.

"That having a dad, because he now wants to be a dad, the children can't have one, because you won't allow it. The law, which represents the will of the people, grants the father of his children what you don't want to give him: the father they never had all these years."

"It's that I can't, Your Honor. I can't trust him with them. He doesn't have the least idea of how to care for them. And what if he takes them away, and I'll never see them again?"

"It won't be like that," the judge responded. "This man will become a dad, little by little. At first, he'll begin seeing the children with a therapist who will supervise the visits; he'll help them get acquainted little by little. Then the therapist will give me a report. As their relationship develops, I'll slowly give them more opportunities, until the father will take them to the park and other places. Finally, we hope we can give him shared custody, that is if he takes advantage of these opportunities. Many fathers don't; they just want to prove a point, then they disappear. But if you, madam, won't cooperate, *you* will lose all custody. That's my order!"

It's the order of the divine Judge that we have him as our heavenly Father, together with his Son as our Eternal Father and Savior. It doesn't matter how long we've been without knowing our heavenly Father; we have the right to have a much better Father than the enemy who has taken over the sole custody of our souls. How and where can we find our true Father? Where is the court where me must file our petition? He is as close as the faintest sigh of your heart, or as the Scripture says, "The word is near you; it is in your mouth and in your heart" (Romans 10:8, EHV). It is not a word that we speak to ourselves. It is the Father's word, "I will not leave you as orphans; I will come to you" (John 14:18, CEB). It is his word of forgiveness that is always present in our lives as a fulfilled promise. The proof is in the resurrection of Christ and the constant ministry of his presence through the Comforter that he gave to us. The Holy Spirit is our Comforter because the Spirit always reminds us of the completed work of Christ on our behalf. What a Father! He fills us with "every spiritual gift" obtained by Christ for us. We don't need to add a jot or a tittle. In fact, we'll spoil it if we add something of our own to it. What Christ did for us is so complete, we lack nothing. "Our cup runneth over"! In the presence of Christ, goodness and mercy follow us all the days of our life, and in the house of our Father, we will live forever.

58

Why Didn't You Report The Abuse Immediately?

> "For all have sinned, and fall short of the glory of God; being justified freely by his grace through the redemption that is in Christ Jesus . . . that he might himself be just, and the justifier of him that hath faith in Jesus" (Romans 3:23-24, 26, ASV).

In sexual abuse cases, it's extremely challenging to discover the truth. At stake is the innocence of young girls as well as the future of a young man who would spend most of his life in jail. A single mother with two girls, thirteen and eleven-years-old, had reported to the police what the girls had confided in her. The problem was she had waited ten months to do it. The girls alleged that the mother's boyfriend had sexually abused them on several occasions, but had not given specific details of what they experienced. The medical tests given by specialists did not show any trace of sexual abuse. But of course, it was months after the alleged events. On the other hand, the girls had changed their story with another detective and claimed they had only been fondled. The girls did not remember exact dates, places, or times. They could have taken the incidents out of some novel.

The defendant's attorney argued credibly that the mother had invented the charges because she discovered in his cell phone, pictures where he was posing intimately with another woman. The attorney reasoned that is why the mother had not reported the alleged abuse. She had not reported it before because she didn't want him to leave her. Or perhaps nothing had happened, and the charges were just a made-up pretext to get rid of that "worthless good for nothing cheater" (as she described him) and put him away in jail for a long time. But if the allegations were made up, then why should the young man have to go to jail for a crime he didn't commit?

Now the district attorney pressed the mother with the same question: Why didn't she report the abuse immediately after the girls told her? Why did she wait for almost a year? To which the mother only answered with silent tears. At any rate, the defense attorney was raising doubt, because the jury could not condemn the defendant unless all twelve jurors were convinced beyond a reasonable doubt.

It was an exceptional case. Usually, in sexual abuse cases, the jury believes the victims. However, in this instance, the jury did not believe the girls' stories or the testimony of the mother. The boyfriend was not guilty of abusing the girls. However, there was more than enough guilt to go around. The boyfriend was guilty of cheating on the mother. But the mother was also guilty of extracting vengeance on the boyfriend by falsely accusing him of actions that would have landed him in jail for many years. The girls were also guilty of conspiring with the mother in slandering the young man.

"For all have sinned and fall short of the glory of God" (Romans 3:23, ASV). Thus, everyone is deserving of divine justice. But divine justice goes beyond finding guilt, condemning, and punishing, because every life is of great value and infinitely precious before God. In our story, the lives of the mother, the boyfriend, the girls – and yes, our very own lives. Divine justice found a way to save the guilty, that is, all of us. Divine justice surprised us with Christ. He bore our guilt, took our punishment, and presented us blameless before God. Yes, "all have sinned and continue to fall short of God's glory." Yet, that damning sentence is followed by a surprising and saving ending: "They are justified by his grace as a gift, through the redemption which is in Christ Jesus, whom God put forward as an expiation by his blood, to be received by faith" (Romans 3:24-25, RSV). If that just sounds like theological jargon to you, what it means is this: You are forgiven. You are not guilty of anything, now or ever. Not because you did anything to deserve it, but because God just loves to forgive. You are declared to be a just person, although you have never done a thing to deserve it. It is all because Christ took your guilt on himself, and gave you his perfect life to substitute for your imperfect record. Call it a conspiracy if you like. Yes, Father, Son, and Holy Spirit have conspired to save you. It's the greatest conspiracy in the history of the universe. And now, against you there's no jury, no attorneys, no accusers, no guilt, no wrath. "There is therefore now no condemnation for those who are in Christ Jesus" (Romans 8:1, RSV), for you have been called to the freedom of God's love (Galatians 5:13).

59
The Program

> "Consider how much love the Father has given to us, that we should be called children of God . . . Everyone who has this hope in Him purifies himself, just as He is pure . . . There is no fear in love, but perfect love casts out fear" (1 John 3:1, 3; 4:18, MEV).

There's a program for parents who've lost custody of their children due to drug abuse crimes. Juvenile Court takes custody of the children. They are placed in a foster home. Then the law grants the father, or mother, the opportunity to reunite with their children. But they have to complete a program of group meetings, therapies, random drug testing, and classes, hold down a job, and have an approved place to live for their children. As they meet the requirements of the program, they step up to another level until they complete all the program requirements. That's when they receive their diploma. But the piece of cardboard means nothing when compared to the joy of once again feeling the embrace of their children.

On a certain occasion, there was a group of parents appearing before the judge, who was reviewing their progress in such a program. "Sir, your report says that you failed an alcohol test. What happened?"

"My grandfather died, and I went out and had some drinks to take away the pain."

To which the judge retorted, "Sir, how many times has alcohol taken away your pain?"

"Well, not once really, because the pain comes back later, and worse than before, and I want to drink even more. That's why I want to quit the program, because it's too demanding."

"But sir, what about your children? Don't you want them back?"

"Your Honor, their mother took them away from me long ago. I've lost hope of ever seeing them again."

"But sir, this is your best chance to get them back again."

"No, no, Your Honor. There's nothing I can do."

"But sir, we can reinstate you in the program; all you have to do is . . ."

The man didn't let the judge finish. He picked up his hat and went out from the courtroom whispering between his teeth, "No one cares about anything; everything is a big waste of time . . ."

What if God had thought the same about us! That it was a waste of time to come and seek to save us! But those thoughts don't enter the mind of God. God in Christ became flesh; he was born in a manger, he took on the humblest and most poverty-ridden life in order to rescue the most helpless and hapless on earth. He was relentlessly persecuted by his own people, humiliated and shamed as the most despicable rebel in all humanity. Then he climbed on a cross to take on the filth of all human sin, in all its hatred, cruelty, and evil. Finally, he rose from the dead to give proof that his love triumphed over evil and death on behalf of every single human being that has ever experienced life on this earth, born or unborn. He offers this gift of forgiveness and eternal life unconditionally, and to the one who least deserves it. "God was in Christ reconciling the world to himself, not counting their trespasses against them . . . God made him, who did not know sin, to become sin for us, so that we might become the righteousness of God in him" (2 Corinthians 5:19, 21, EHV). The gift of this righteousness includes two amazing blessings. First, it's the gift of eternal life; for in his body, Christ took on himself every curse of the law against our life, thus freeing us from sin and its consequence of death. The second blessing is to enfold us with his love during our life here and now. Under the shadow of his wings, we are renewed, cared for, protected, and above all, loved as no one else could love us. "See the kind of love the Father has given us that we should be called children of God, and that is what we are! ... Everyone who has this hope purifies himself just as Jesus is pure" (1 John 3:1, 3, MEV). "There is no fear in love, but complete love drives out fear" (1 John 4:18, MEV). You have nothing to fear. You'll never want to quit that program. It's for your life now and throughout eternity!"

60

I Blew It!

> "Truly I tell you, unless a grain of wheat falls to the ground and dies, it remains by itself. But if it dies, it produces much fruit" (John 12:24, CSB).

"I'm going to steal this six-pack." With these words, the teenage plunked a six-pack of beer on the register counter of a convenience store. Then looking intently at the cashier, he grabbed the pack and went out the door whistling some nonsense tune. He got inside his car, made an obscene gesture with one hand, and waved goodbye to the cashier. She immediately memorized the license plate. In less than an hour, the honest thief was at the police station.

Now, days after his last heist, he sat chin in hands at the Juvenile Hall interview room, together with his mother and defense attorney. The lawyer spoke first. "Chris, I can't believe it! What were you thinking? Don't you remember? You were already on probation. In just one week, you'll turn eighteen; the judge was going to dismiss your case if you didn't get into any more trouble. Chris, you had just one week left! Now your record is going to have that conviction, and it will follow you as an adult."

I was translating each phrase for the mother. The lawyer continued, "Have you already told your mother what happened?" And then to the mother, "Madam, has he told you anything? Do you know what happened?"

The mother's face went pale with unbelief and confusion. "I don't know anything; he hasn't told me anything."

The lawyer continued, "Chris, six months ago you were here for an identical case. But the judge gave you probation instead of locking you up when he saw your high school graduation picture. We were all so proud of you. The police report says that you confessed to more than thirty such thefts. Now, what do you want me to tell the judge?"

Looking down at his shoes, he simply answered, "I blew it!"

That's what, beginning with Adam, we have all done, "Blew it!" We have ruined a beautiful planet with irreversible damage to the air, land, and seas. With our hatred and greed, we have reaped wars, divisions, killings, theft of lands, displacement of millions of people from their towns and homes, exploitation of natural resources at the cost of the earth itself, jealousy and resentment among families, acts of vengeance, trampling of people's rights, and countless injustice from the family to nation against nation. It seems strange, but in the newborn's innocent cry, you can already hear the announcement: "Here's a new sinner! My father was Adam, an unbeliever, liar, and disloyal!" If you pay attention, you'll hear more: "I'm going to give my parents headaches, I'm going to frustrate them, I'm going to disappoint my teachers, and whether they catch me or not, I'm going to disobey countless times, I'm going to tell lies, I'll even try misdemeanors and felonies!" Until a different announcement was heard about the birth of a most unique child: "For to us a child is born. To us a son is given. The authority to rule will rest on his shoulders. He will be named: Wonderful Counselor, Mighty God, Everlasting Father, Prince of Peace" (Isaiah 9:6, EHV). His first cry made another announcement: "I'm going to put an end to sin's rule over humanity. I'll live and die in their place. I'll always love and obey according to my Father's will. I will climb on a cross and take humanity's weight of sin on my body. I will reconcile all things in heaven and earth to the Father and myself." And then, he made a vow: "Look, I've come to do your will, God. This has been written about me in the scroll" (Hebrews 10:7, CEB).

That will of the Father was for that child to become our Substitute in life and in death. From his first breath until his last—and it was so. Instead of "blowing it," he put together a holy and pure life, abounding in obedience, holiness, love, patience, and kindness. Everything that we destroyed when we "blew it," he put together again. And, how did he do it? "Truly I tell you, unless a grain of wheat falls to the ground and dies, it remains by itself. But if it dies, it produces much fruit" (John 12:24, CEB). You no longer have to regret what you did and just look down at your shoes. Chin up. Look forward to his life. His life is yours, and by faith alone. No one will take it away from you. "I have come that they may have life, and have it abundantly" (John 10:10, NIV).

61

She Came For Wool, But Got Shorn In The Process

> "Like a lamb led to the slaughter and like a sheep silent before her shearers, he did not open his mouth" (Isaiah 53:7, CSB). "But these are written that you may believe that Jesus is the Messiah, the Son of God, and that by believing you may have life in his name" (John 20:31, CSB).

From the judicial bench the judge summarized the case: "This is Mrs. Delores Poorme's claim against Mr. Gether Offmyback. The petitioner is asking for an increase in child support from the respondent. She claims the $100.00 monthly support from her ex is not enough. She's not working currently, and three months ago she gave birth to another child." The judge then addressed Mrs. Poorme. "Madam, are you currently working?"

"No, Your Honor. My home is my work. I have five children: his three kids and two with my new husband."

The judge continued, "And does your current husband work?"

"Yes, he does. He makes good money. He does know how to take care of a woman. That's why I quit work."

The judge pressed on, "But do you suffer from some chronic illness, or some disability that doesn't allow you to work?"

"No, Your Honor, I am in good health."

The judge wasn't done. "But then, how do you expect your ex-husband to work and provide for the children? Don't you expect the same from yourself? Aren't they your children as well?"

She had a ready answer. “Yes, but it’s that now I have two children with my new husband.”

But the judge was also ready: “That’s fine. But because you have two children in your new relationship, do your other children stop being your responsibility? No madam, I’m giving you sixty days to find a job. From that date on, let’s say you’ll be paid minimum wage, and with your husband’s great earnings . . . here’s the amount given by the automatic calculation according to the custody formula . . . You’ll have to pay your ex-husband the amount of $150.00 dollars a month.” As the woman marched out of the courtroom, I heard someone whisper, “She came for wool, but got shorn in the process.”

We could debate the fairness or unfairness of the judge’s ruling. But in God’s great judgment throne, things were thrown upside down. He was the one who came for the sheep, and got shorn in the process. Scripture says, “Like a lamb he was led to the slaughter, and like a sheep that is silent in front of its shearers, he did not open his mouth” (Isaiah 53:7, CSB). How did we take him to the slaughter? We punished him for loving us! We nailed to the cross what he came to give us: his life! We rejected him as our Substitute. We? We don’t need a Substitute—perhaps just someone to give us a push every now and then. Someone to tell us how well we are doing. But we have great human qualities with which to please God, don’t we? We don’t want those going to waste. Gotta use them. But a Substitute? That only tells us that what we have to offer isn’t good enough. So if he’s offering to be our Substitute, let’s take him to the slaughter. He’s an offense to our spiritual human capacity to overcome, to transform ourselves. That’s all we need, the right steps to overcome our faults, and present ourselves as overcomers before God! But all he did was to show us the steps to the cross, and then asked us to follow him there. Not good. Things would have gone better for him had he not been so extreme. And offering himself as our Substitute before God was a little extreme, don’t you think?

But even though he knew we would reject him as our greatest gift, he gave himself to forgive our rejection, our unbelief, our pride, and even our pious spiritual pride. “He was despised and rejected by men . . . and we thought nothing of him. Surely he was taking up our weaknesses” (Isaiah 53:3, 4, EHV). So we cut him off the land of the living; we sheared him of his life.

But he allowed himself to get sheared, and out of that wool, he fashioned for us a robe of righteousness, which substitutes for our own, because our own is worthless. He persevered against our unbelief, against our stubbornness, against our fickleness, which insisted on having something of our own to cover our sins. He saw the absurdity of our thinking that sought to cover sin with sin, imperfection with more imperfection. He had mercy on us, "For He knows our frame. He remembers that we are dust" (Psalm 103:14, EHV). So what did he get for all he did for us? The joy of coming before the Father and saying, "Here I am with the children [you] have given me" (Isaiah 8:18, CSB). and not one is missing. And by grace through faith alone, you and I are among them!

62

Easy As Pie

> "He went a little farther, fell on his face, and prayed. He said, "My Father, if it is possible, let this cup pass from me. Yet not as I will, but as you will" (Matthew 26:39, EHV).

Juvenile Hall judges have several options when punishing minors for various types of criminal behavior. They can order lock up, supervised probation, community service, fines, a combination of these, or some other corrective action designed to educate rather than to punish.

Today a fourteen-year-old boy appeared before the judge accused of shoplifting four beers from a convenience store. The police report noted that it was a cold winter evening. The young man entered the store wearing a long dark coat, and walked along the aisle leading to the cold beers. The security camera showed that he opened the fridge doors and seconds later stepped back. He then walked back to the cashier, paid for a pack of gum, and walked briskly to a parked van where three other young men waited. Seconds later, as the van backed up, two patrol cars closed in and stopped the getaway. Three boys darted out of the car and got away. The fourth, the protagonist of our story, also tried to get away, but as he started to run, the bottom of his large coat got caught in the door. As he tugged on it, the bottles of beer fell on the asphalt and rolled away as the police agents approached. Now, days later, he was facing the judge.

"Young man, whatever got into you? Why did you lift those beers?"

After a few seconds, a faint smile came across his face. Timidly he said, "Because it was easy as pie, Your Honor."

"Easy?" grunted the judge. "Here's what I'll do for you. You must write 1,000 times 'As easy as pie, Your Honor.' Use a lined notebook just for this purpose. Both sides of the page. On each line. Number them. You have thirty days. I'm sure it'll be as easy as pie for you. It's only thirty-three lines per day. No cheating with photocopies or having someone help you. I'll be checking the handwriting. Good-bye."

Thirty days later the boy showed up with a worn notebook in hand. "Well, young man. Was it as easy as pie?" asked the judge in good humor.

"Your Honor, I never thought an 'easy as pie' would turn out to be so hard," answered the boy respectfully. "Thanks for the lesson." In the back of the room, his parents had a great big smile.

Beginning with our first parents, we have all used a version of the same excuse. "It happened just because, well, the woman you gave me, made it easy for me to eat of the fruit," said Adam. "The serpent you made, made it easy for me, I ate the fruit just because, well it deceived me, and I ate." "It was just easy for me to tell that little white lie." "I couldn't help it, I just cheated on the time sheet." "It just happened that my eyes drifted to my classmate's test, and I saw the answer." It's easy as pie for human behavior to do what's forbidden, to deceive, to harm, just because.

But it was extremely difficult for him who had to pay for our "I just couldn't help it," or "things just happened." It was so excruciatingly painful to take on our death, our guilt, our sins, that he sweated drops of blood there in Gethsemane. "My Father, if it's possible, free me from taking this bitter cup; but not as I will, but as you will" (Matthew 26:39, EHV). But the real difficult part was yet ahead. His worst suffering was when he became sin for us. His soul pain was such that he felt abandoned by the Father. In extreme anguish he cried, "My God, my God, why have you abandoned me?" (Matthew 27:46, CSB).

If the heavenly Judge were to ask us to write, "I sinned just because I felt like it," how many times would we have to write it? If the oceans were made of ink, they would go dry before we made it past the first page. But we're not given that task. It is enough that he wrote, "I forgive you because I love you" with his blood, there on the cross. If you look closely, you'll see your name written there. So, take a notebook, get started and write: "I've been forgiven; I worship you!"

63

If You Don't Sign, I Will

> He went a little farther, fell on his face, and prayed. He said, "My Father, if it is possible, let this cup pass from me. Yet not as I will, but as you will" (Matthew 26:39, EHV).

The couple was appearing for one of their last hearings in their complicated divorce proceedings. The judge had already granted them marital dissolution. The only document missing was the final distribution of goods. Soon after their marriage, the couple had bought a house, which rapidly acquired a significant amount of equity. The judge had ruled that both parties sign a writ authorizing a real estate agent to sell the house. He had also ordered that the writ be signed and filed with the court within fourteen days. Now, ninety days later, the former wife petitioned the court for relief since her former husband had not signed the authorization. A buyer had offered the full selling price, but the sale was not executed because the husband had not signed. The woman was furious.

"He has always been like this, Your Honor. He promises, then goes back on his word, now this good opportunity is gone."

The judge then asked the man, "Do you remember I gave you two weeks to sign? Why didn't you sign?"

"It's that I had to leave the country. My grandmother, who was like a mother to me, was gravely ill, and I had to go see her."

"It's a lie, Your Honor," interrupted the former wife. "He doesn't want to sell the property because I'll get half of it, but half of it belongs to me!"

"Look sir," added the judge. "It seems to me more than a coincidence that your grandmother gets sick just when a buyer became available, and offering a great price. And you didn't leave the country until eleven days after my order. Since you are not willing to sign, I'm taking judicial discretion to authorize my clerk to sign all documents related to the sale of your house. So ordered!

Many years back, God gave his law, and asked Israel to sign. The people said yes, it would do everything asked of them, for the good of the planet, of their neighbor, and for the glory of God. It signed, but the ink on the paper went blank! That's the state of humanity. In some way or another, we have all signed stating that we will be good persons, respectful, considerate, honest. But when put to the test, we do just the opposite. Our future went dark; we lost everything. Until Christ came and said, "I'll sign on behalf of all the promise breakers." But the naysayers said, "They'll despise you for your mercy; they'll even nail you to a cross! Others will just take you for granted; they won't care what you did. Don't do it."

But Christ responded, "I don't do it because of what they may think, or if they value my sacrifice or not. I do it because I love them." (John 3:16). Some will listen to me, they will believe. I do this for those who need it the most, for those who fully distrust in themselves. I do it for the weakest, the most frail. I do it for those who have tried everything and failed. I do it for them. It's for them that I sign my promise. "For the Son of Man came to seek and to save the lost" (Luke 19:10, EHV).

And it was so. He signs only for those whose hands tremble with fear, with guilt, for the hard blows of disappointment they've received in life. He signs only for those who have bad handwriting, for the illiterate in the faith. He only signs for those who can only place an "X" beside their name. He signs only for those who can only whisper to him, "Please, you sign my name, and I together with my entire house will be saved!" He promised, and then fulfilled. There, on the cross, he was signing with his own blood, and in our place. And as Judge of the universe, he signed guaranteeing your eternal salvation. Is there something else you'd like for him to do?

64

He Doesn't Let Suffering Get in The Way of Love!

> And when he finds it, he joyfully puts it on his shoulders and goes home. Then he calls his friends and neighbors together and says, 'Rejoice with me; I have found my lost sheep.' I tell you that in the same way there will be more rejoicing in heaven over one sinner who repents than over ninety-nine righteous persons who do not need to repent (Luke 15:5-7, EHV).

"And, for how long do you want this restraining order?" asked the judge. How many times have judges asked that question! On the answer hangs the future of entire families, relationships, hates, quarrels, resentments, and thousands of silent sighs. In this matter, the petitioner was a sixty-five-year-old woman, requesting a Stay-away Order from her thirty-two-year-old son. "Oh my, I don't know," was the mother's uncertain and tearful answer.

"That's fine," answered the judge rather impatiently. "I'll give you the maximum; it's for five years. Take a seat; we'll give you the order in a few minutes."

"Nooooo!" The tears changed into a high decibel plea. "Don't make it for so long! My husband will die without seeing him!"

"Then, shall I make it for four or three years? Look madam, the allegations of your son's abuse against you and your husband fill up many pages of the court file; they could all be charged as felonies. He steals from you, pushes you around, and breaks windows and doors to get in looking for cash. That's how he supports his drug addiction. This is your chance to get long-term protection. The police will come immediately to your house if you have this standing order."

"Noooo, Your Honor,' repeated the mother. "One year is enough. My husband is eighty-one years old; if he doesn't see him, I know he'll die soon. He suffers so much for that boy, but doesn't let his suffering get in the way of his love for him!"

"Well then, it'll be for one year. Come back if you need to extend it. Don't hesitate to come back sooner if you need more help."

God had to deal with precisely such a situation with the human race. He suffered a great deal because of us. He saw our rebellious spirit, our betrayal, disloyalty, and perfidy. We were addicted to our evil; we robbed him of the honor due to his name. We slandered him as unjust, cruel, unnecessary, irrelevant, and out of date. We denied his paternity, even his existence. But our worst claim was to presume on our wisdom saying, "We are our own creation. We emerged spontaneously from the dust of the earth."

God's reaction? Not for an instant did God think of abandoning us. Rather, like the good shepherd, he came to look for his lost sheep. And after a life of trials, persecution, and temptations from the manger to Calvary's cruelty, he finally found us stuck in our own mud—the mud we had claimed had given spontaneous birth to us! "And when he found us, he joyfully placed us on his shoulders. And while going home he called his friends and neighbors together and saying, 'Rejoice with me; I have found my lost sheep.' I tell you that in the same way there will be more rejoicing in heaven over one sinner who repents than over ninety-nine righteous persons who do not need to repent" (Luke 15:5-7, EHV). It's because he cannot live without us that he suffers our defiant spirit toward him. Nonetheless, he never lets his suffering get in the way of his love for us. He rejoices not just when he hears our voice, but his joy is complete when he has us by his side. That's how Jesus the Christ deals with your life and mine. "This is love: not that we loved God, but that he loved us and sent his Son as an atoning sacrifice for our sins" (1 John 4:10, EHV).

65

That Wasn't Grace, That Was Just A Scare

> "There is no fear in love. But perfect love drives out fear, because fear has to do with punishment" (1 John 4:18, NIV). "This is how we know what love is: Jesus Christ laid down his life for us" (1 John 3:16, NIV).

"Sir, four weeks ago I ordered you to attend twelve AA meetings. Here you bring me signatures for only ten. You are missing two. I ordered you to go to these meetings due to your second DUI conviction. Or, will I have to lock you up for you to learn how to count?"

The man was shaking. "It's that I have an explanation, Your Honor. I want to talk to an attorney."

"Alright, talk to the attorney, but for now you are staying here. You are not to leave the courtroom without my permission!"

The man's story was fascinating, yet credible. "I had a cold. In the evening I stopped by my sister's house where I fell asleep watching TV. I woke up at 1:30 in the morning with a burning sore throat. In the kitchen, I found a spray for sore throat pain. Since I had so much pain that I couldn't even swallow, I sprayed the back of my throat four times. I then drove my car home, and on the way, someone ran into me at the corner. The cop came, and ordered me out of the car because he could smell alcohol on my breath. He made me blow several times into the little machine and told me that I had been drinking. He then took me to the police station. I really don't know why or what happened."

"What's the name of that throat spray?" asked the lawyer. When he heard the name, he said, "That spray has a high alcohol content. You literally covered the back of your throat with pure alcohol, and that's what you blew into the Breathalyzer. I'll talk to the judge and tell him your story."

But the judge didn't buy it. He reminded the defendant that it was his second DUI (Driving Under the Influence of alcohol), and that he was missing two AA meetings. "I'll have to lock you up," the judge told him.

The man's face slowly was covered with tears. "But my three children, Your Honor."

"You should have thought about them before you got to drinking and driving."

At that point, I had to leave the courtroom. Days later, I saw the judge in the hallway and asked him what had happened to the man with the sore throat spray. "I let him go!"

"What? You gave him grace?"

"Grace, nothing," he answered with a wry laugh. "I just scared him! Sometimes I have to scare people into compliance!"

Many think the same about God. That religion is only good for scaring people, but once they get over their fear, they go back to the same; they quit believing. They are not far from the truth. But the truth is that Scripture says that, "perfect love drives out fear" (1 John 4:18, NIV). Also, "This is how we know what love is: Jesus Christ laid down his life for us" (1 John 3:16, NIV). The judge in our story was neither unjust nor mean for frightening the accused. He was acting according to the law, and that is why he was using the law to scare him into compliance.

But with respect to God and humanity, Jesus the Christ wedged himself between the law and us. From there he cried out, "Let the just and righteous punishment of the law fall on me, and not on these sinners who don't know what they're doing!" And that is why he climbed on that cross in your place and mine. There he felt all our fear, our regrets, our sighs of repentance, and our terror over what our sins may have done to others. He took on all that fear that we feel when we are all alone and see ourselves as we are. He felt the fears of all humanity pressing against his own soul, in order to free us from all our fears. Whoever understands this will understand how much he is loved. That love shown on the cross, casts out our fear. But the irony is that God has to love us, not scare us, in order to bring us to himself. That kind of love is even scary. But we don't die of fright. The fear turns into love, and his love gives us life, and life eternal!

66

The Unfaithful Witness

> "For God so loved the world that he gave his one and only Son, that whoever believes in him shall not perish but have eternal life . . . For Christ also suffered once for sins, the righteous for the unrighteous, to bring you to God" (John 3:16; 1 Peter 3:18, NIV).

The evaluator's report was not flattering for the mother. When the children were interviewed, they said that, "mom was drinking lots of beer" at home; she drank when she drove, she drove too fast, she belted them, and mistreated them with bad words. The father said that everything was true, that he felt sorry for the mother, but she was simply out of control. He was petitioning for full custody of the children. He conceded visits to the mother, but only with a paid supervisor.

"Have you personally witnessed the mother mistreat the children?" asked the judge.

"Yes, Your Honor, many times, and just as often I've had to intervene."

"They are all lies, Your Honor," replied the mother.

"Don't interrupt," commanded the judge. "Do you have any other witness of such abuse?"

"Yes, she's outside. She's the manager of the apartments where I live."

"No, Your Honor," interrupted the mother once more. "She's the cause of all our problems! She is his lover. She's the reason we separated!"

"Call her in," ordered the judge rather emotionless.

Testifying under oath, she claimed that on several occasions, she had seen the mother push, shove, and strike the children. The judge then asked her, "Do you currently have something personal or an intimate relationship with the petitioner?"

"Nothing like that at all, Your Honor. I keep a professional relationship with all the renters." At that, the mother broke out in tears.

The judge ruled on behalf of the father. He ordered him to wait outside in the hallway. The court orders would be delivered to him. A few minutes later, the judge's clerk with papers in hand left the courtroom. When she came back, she was ashen faced. With trembling voice, she told the judge, "That woman was lying. As soon as I gave him the papers, he called out to her, "Look, my love, here are all the papers we wanted."

Before God's judgment seat, Jesus the Christ is completely the opposite. He testifies against himself, and gives witness in our favor. The Father asks him, "Is it true, my Son, that you've committed all the sins of _______________?" (Put your name on the blank).

"Yes, my Father. I leave nothing out, I plead guilty for all of them. On his behalf and on behalf for every single human being, I plead guilty. I committed all the sins and faults they have all committed. I am sin itself. In order to take away sin, you have to allow me to die on behalf of them all. When I die, all sin dies with me, and forever."

This is sometimes called the "glorious exchange." At the cross, Jesus Christ took on his person all the sins, hatreds, and inhumanities all human beings committed against each other, and against the planet, God's creation. In that exchange, all his righteousness, holiness, perfection, and love is put to the account of every single human being. All are included regardless of race, gender, socioeconomic status, color, or anything else. Since their record is filled completely with the righteousness of Christ, there is no room at all for any of their own sins. They don't fit. The life of Christ has filled it all. This must be thought through several times before it's fully understood. It's divine logic; it's not human reasoning. But if logical thinking doesn't help you figure it out, try faith. "For God so loved the world that he gave his one and only Son, that whoever believes in him shall not perish but have eternal life . . . For Christ also suffered once for sins, the righteous for the unrighteous, to bring you to God" (John 3:16; 1 Peter 3:18, NIV). Faith in this true witness is all we need, and the righteousness of Christ is all that will keep us alive throughout eternity!

67

The Truth And Nothing But The Truth

> "The reason I was born and came into the world is to testify to the truth. Everyone on the side of truth listens to me" (John 18:37, NIV).

The woman approached to be sworn in by the clerk before stepping on the witness stand to give her testimony. As instructed by the clerk, she raised her right hand while I interpreted: "Do you solemnly swear that the testimony you shall give before this court shall be the truth, the whole truth, and nothing but the truth?"

The charges and allegations were extremely serious. Her husband (the grandfather) had been accused by the nine-year-old granddaughter of having fondled her while she slept. The district attorney alleged that the incidents had occurred during the girl's visits to her grandparents' home. Now the grandmother was about to give her sworn testimony. The defense attorney alleged that the girl was lying because the girl's mother and her grandmother had put words in her mouth. She also alleged that the motive for the false allegations was because those grandparents had excluded both the mother and the girl from a large inheritance of goods and properties.

During the examination, the district attorney insisted with the same question, "How many times a month had the girl visited her home?" It was difficult to translate the grandmother's response. She hesitated and stammered; she began again, only to falter and stagger again, finally answering almost in a whisper. Sometimes she answered, "Once or twice a month." Then again, "Two times every six weeks." What was the truth? The girl had already given her testimony. She admitted on the stand (after examination from the judge that she knew the difference between the truth and a lie) that her mother and the other grandma had told her to say that the grandpa had fondled her. That the accusation was not the truth, but when the detectives had offered her an ice cream cone, she had said that yes, he had touched her in her private parts, but just a little bit. But she really hadn't told the truth. So, what was the truth?

It is said that Diogenes, the ancient Greek, had walked the streets during sunlight hours with a lit torch. When he was asked why he was doing such nonsense, he would respond with great lament, "I am looking for one honest man on the face of the earth." But the only honest man who has ever risen in answer to that search is Jesus of Nazareth. But few believe him. Before Pilate, who had the power to send him to the cross or set him free, Jesus said, "The reason I was born and came into the world is to testify to the truth. Everyone on the side of truth listens to me" (John 18:37, NIV). In response Pilate had uttered the infamous phrase, "What is truth?" But Pilate was looking at the truth straight into its face, and yet he couldn't see it. What was that truth? That same Jesus, whose blood Pilate would soon symbolically wash off his hands, was about to go to the cross to die for his sin of unbelief. The truth that Jesus was about to shed his blood to forgive him for the unjust sentence he was about to join at that moment, "Let him be crucified." Jesus went to the cross to suffer our unbelief, our lack of faith, for living a lie before those around us, for wanting to wash responsibility off our hands for our neighbor.

Who truly lives the truth at life's every moment? Who hasn't twisted the truth a tiny bit, just to look a bit more pious and responsible? Who hasn't lied in answering the simplest question: "How are you?" At the exposed untruth of our life, Jesus intervenes with the truth of his life, the only sincere, honest, and infinitely virtuous person who has ever set foot on this earth! And when we believe in him—that is the only truth God looks upon when he sets his eyes on us. He is the truth, the whole truth, and nothing but the truth. He already raised his hand, gave his sworn testimony on the cross, that his life would be a sufficient gift in exchange for our untruth. He didn't ask us if we believed him or if we wanted it, for we would have told a lie. He did it only out of love for us. Ah, and don't forget. His whole inheritance is yours as well. You didn't get left out. It's nothing but the truth.

68

Three Questions

> "Christ loved the church and gave himself up for her . . . to present her to himself as a radiant church, without stain or wrinkle or any other blemish, but holy and blameless" (Ephesians 5:25, 27, NIV).

It doesn't matter the age, or years of marriage, or if they've had children together, or what goods they have in common. The moment the judge declares, "You are no longer married; from here on, you are single people" creates a solemn hush over the courtroom. After a few seconds, papers rustle on the table, some sighs of relief are heard, and someone whispers: "Congratulations, congratulations." Chairs squeak as they are pushed back; bodies that once walked hand in hand now avoid each other as they exit. They are sobering moments. Quite a contrast from the wedding day. A church wedding. The inside of the church so thoughtfully decorated: all the flowers symbolic of the freshness of the couple's love. Surrounded by friends, relatives, bridesmaids in beautiful dresses, young men in tuxedos, romantic music in the background, the groom elegant and radiant with his smile, and, of course, the joyous bride in her splendid dress.

At the divorce table, the courtroom is austere—no flowers, no decorations, none present at the wedding are here. The tick-tock of the large wall clock provides the background music. Instead of the priest taking the marriage vows, it is now the judge asking three questions. "Have irreconcilable differences arisen between you?" If either one answers yes, the judge continues. "Would it be helpful if the court provided marriage therapy to work toward reconciliation?" If either one answers no, the judge continues. "Is the marriage relationship so broken that it is beyond any remedy?" If either one answers yes, the judge then declares: "You are no longer married, you are free to live as single persons." Are these the same two people that vowed eternal love to each other? Who kissed tenderly at the altar? Enjoyed a passionate honeymoon under the stars? Who built a home together? Are these the ones who raised several children together, celebrated their birthdays and triumphs? What happened? What causes led to this heartbreaking outcome? To those divorced, these questions have been dealt with, and the parties moved on the best they could.

But a divorce from God? Sounds outrageous. But it's true. Humanity has filed for divorce from God. The reasons? Humankind accuses God of being an absent husband. Many believe he doesn't even exist. Yet, they blame God (although they deny his existence) for all the evils of the world: wars, droughts, famines, pandemics, illnesses, hatreds, unmanageable children, birth defects, many religions, poverty, global warming, hurricanes, airplane accidents, shipwrecks, and so much more. Humanity wants a divorce, and now. But while we complain, argue, and accuse God and those who believe in God, we don't realize we are still loved and in his arms. While we blame God for placing us in a meaningless universe, and that we are nothing but stardust, our true destiny is "a new heavens and a new earth in which righteousness dwells" (2 Peter 3:13, ESV). That's why he doesn't buy into our divorce petition. His answer to the questions is: "I will not forget you! See, I have engraved you on the palms of my hands" (Isaiah 49:15-16, NIV). I can't abandon you, my creation, the work of my love. My heart is moved with love within me; my compassion burns for your redemption.

God's love opposes our divorce petition. But he didn't intervene with any writing on tablets of stone, not even on the heart of flesh. It was his heart of flesh manifested in Jesus Christ that offered his life on the cross in protest to our divorce petition. On the cross, he became all our unbelief, contrary desires, hatreds, anger, and vindictive spirit. He took it all on himself. There is no evil manifestation in our being that was not placed on the purity of his soul. Why? To present us, not tomorrow, but today, before the eternal Judge as his bride: "a radiant church, without stain or wrinkle or any other blemish, but holy and blameless" (Ephesians 5:27, NIV). That is how the eternal Judge ignores our divorce petition, our complaints, our blaming him for all our evils. The music to the wedding feast has never stopped. It is still playing. "Praise the Lord with the harp; make music to him on the ten-stringed lyre . . . The Lord loves righteousness and justice; the earth is full of his unfailing love" (Psalm 33:2, 5, NIV). Let's tear up our divorce petitions, for it is his love that through the cross has conquered our hearts.

69

He Shows Up Asking For Our Daughter

> "But the fruit of the spirit is love, joy, peace, patience, kindness, goodness, faithfulness, gentleness, and self-control. Against such things there is no law" (Galatians 5:22-23, NIV).

The woman petitioned a Stay-away order protecting her fifteen-year-old daughter, her husband, and herself. I was there to translate for the hearing. No one said a word while the judge read the petition. "And where is the respondent?" asked the judge.

"I don't know, said the woman. "He knew he had to be here. I believe Your Honor has the Proof of Service."

"That's true; let's go on with the hearing. Madam, do you swear that what you wrote here is the truth?"

"Yes, Your Honor."

"Let's deal with the matter then. Madam, you say here that this man 'comes looking for your fifteen-year-old daughter?'"

"That's true, Your Honor."

"But he's thirty-two years old," added the judge as he continued. "And exactly what do you mean when you say 'he comes looking for our daughter?'"

"Well, my husband and I are sitting out there on the porch, and he comes across the street all drunk, and he tells us he wants to marry her. But I tell him, 'Do you realize she is a minor? Do you know what you're saying?'"

"Well, and then what does he do?" asked the judge.

"He turns around and leaves, but comes back later knocking at the door and saying the same thing. He lives just across the street. My daughter is terrified of him, and so are we. We don't know what to do."

"Is this your daughter with you in the courtroom, and your husband?"

"Yes, they are, Your Honor." As I glanced their way, the girl hardly looked like she had entered puberty, looking more like a girl in late childhood rather than an adolescent.

"Madam, I grant you the restraining order for at least five years. We will deliver the respondent a copy. You are to take a copy to the nearest police station. Even if you just see him crossing the street to your house, call the police right away. With this restraining order, they will arrest him right away."

A few weeks later I was looking at the calendar call list for new arraignments, and I recognized the man's name. He had been arrested for violating the restraining order.

Not quite the suitor we'd want for our daughter either. But if the mother had not acted quickly, "familiarity breeds contempt," or carelessness. Many times, the behavior of suitors like this is normalized, carelessness takes over, and tragedy strikes.

The man's behavior reminds me of the men of Sodom. Like the man of our story, they lived in constant lust. When two angels sent from God to save Lot from Sodom's impending destruction, the men surrounded Lot's house. But their intention was to force Lot to bring the visitors out to them, so they could rape them publicly. Lot's response was not much different when he offered to bring out his young virgin daughters in exchange for the men. The two angels had to strike the men with blindness. Then, even blinded, they groped for the door to force their entry. That was the moral muck in which Lot and his family lived. But it was God's intention to save Lot and his family. Scripture records that "the Lord was merciful to them" (Genesis 19:16, NIV). The Hebrew word used here for "merciful" comes from a word that means "extreme desire to show mercy."

So in the story we have two extreme desires clashing with each other. The extreme desire of Sodom's men to do harm to Lot's family and his guests clashing with God's extreme desire to show pity to

Lot and his family. God's extreme desire to save goes into the mud pool of Sodom to save those who believe in that mercy. And even though Lot's faith and the faith of his family was so weak that the angels had to drag them out of the city, God's extreme desire to save brought them out with a strong hand. God's desire to save us is so extreme he came down into this planet, which could well be called Sodom – for its injustices – planted a cross so that in the extremity of our evil desires and our blindness, we would gropingly find him. Yes, we may think we find him, but it is he who has found us. The angels knew where Sodom was. And they take us out of our burning cities – the cities of our own creation within ourselves – to the safety of Christ's person. There he says, "I will not leave you nor forsake you" (Joshua 1:5, NKJV).

70

I'm Your Attorney; I'm Going To Resolve Your Case

> "My children, I write these things to you so that you will not sin. If anyone does sin, we have an Advocate before the Father: Jesus Christ, the Righteous One" (1 John 2:1, EHV).

The fourteen-year-old entered the interview room with his parents and attorney. Although the boy looked fit and physically mature for his age, his face had turned pale. His parents also looked well educated, yet their faces betrayed their fear. At the desk, the lawyer was reading the file. He finally looked up, looking at the parents and the boy.

With a fleeting smile on his face, he said, "Look, the young woman's accusations are serious, but trust me, I am going to resolve your case."

"How serious?" asked the mother, still ashen faced.

"If he were not a minor, he'd be facing at least fifteen years in the state penitentiary for these allegations. But trust me, I am your attorney; I am going to resolve your case."

Next, it was the father who broke the silence: "And what are the options?"

"Sir, the young man could plead guilty today. He would receive a six-month lock up sentence in Juvenile Hall, followed by three years of probation, or until he turns eighteen. But I am your attorney, I am going to resolve your case."

"And what if he doesn't plead guilty today?" inquired the mother.

"I am going to request the judge to postpone the arraignment for sixty days. I'll give the pretext that I need to investigate the evidence and allegations. Meanwhile, find a sexual therapy counselor for the boy and have him go to at least three sessions a week. He can't miss any classes at school, and must get his grades up. But remember, I am your attorney, I am going to resolve your case."

Not once did the attorney scold the young man or humiliate him for his behavior; nor did he censure him for his offensive conduct against his classmate. Neither did the young man say a word. He just heard – and trusted – his attorney's word: "I am going to resolve your case."

Sixty days later, the young man was back. The lawyer went right to the point: "Your Honor, during the last sixty days this young man's conduct has been above reproach. He has attended twenty-four sessions of sexual therapy for minors, he has improved his grades, and he has not missed a single day of school. Thus, I request that this matter be dismissed."

"So ordered," ruled the judge.

Outside the courtroom the parents and the boy embraced the lawyer, "You were right; you resolved our case."

Scripture affirms, "we have an Advocate before the Father: Jesus Christ, the Righteous One" (1 John 2:1, EHV). Doubtless, he resolved our case: "There is now no condemnation for those who are in Christ Jesus" (Romans 8:1, EHV). In Old Testament times, Moses served as that advocate between Israel and God. There was a crisis when God's wrath was going to visit Israel for their idolatry. But Moses pleaded before God, "But now, please forgive their sin—but if not, then blot me out of the book you have written" (Exodus, 32:32, NIVUK).

That was Moses advocating, interceding, and attempting to resolve Israel's case. But God rejected that noble request. It would not have worked, for Moses, too, was a sinner. God's response was: "Whoever has sinned against me I will blot out of my book" (Exodus 32:33, NIVUK), which meant Moses, too, would be blotted out of God's book. Even Moses, for all his piety, patience, and virtues needed an intercessor. Our designated attorney, sent from God, was "Jesus Christ, the righteous" (1 John 2:1, EHV). He did what no other attorney, earthly or divine, could have done. He became sin for each one of us, so that he himself would be blotted out of the book of life! That's the reason for his desperate cry on the cross, "My God, my God, Why have you forsaken me?" (Matthew 27:46, NIV). That is supreme and unique Advocate intercession. He not only pleaded for us as Moses did, but by becoming the sin that we are, he received the righteous wrath of God that we deserve, on his holy being. Then he declares us as righteous as he is, an infinite gift there is no way we deserve. We were not given a probationary period in which to prove ourselves worthy before the Judge. Even our best compliance would have been declared faulty, for it would have been given from a sinful nature. Yes, it's given to us by grace alone and received through faith alone. He completely resolved our case before God, once and for all. He will never have to become sin for us again. With one sacrifice it was complete, and forever. He's right there before us. And when we celebrate it with his presence in the bread and wine, let's hug him joyfully for such a great and imperishable gift!

71

I Am Andrés Ricardo Mattias[1]

> "God was reconciling the world to himself through Christ, by not counting people's sins against them. He has trusted us with this message of reconciliation" (2 Corinthians 5:19, CEB).

"I am not Andrés Ricardo Mattías; I am Andrés Melardo Mattias, Please tell the judge: I am not responsible for these charges. I don't know why I am here."

When the court clerk heard it, she spoke out, "Your Honor, there are some defendants that always claim there's a mistake in their names. They give false names, or add other last names, to avoid the charges. Look at the signatures on file. We don't get fooled here that easily."

Even though the charges were not that serious, they had immigration consequences, and the man could be deported if he pleaded guilty, or was declared guilty. The risk was serious. Once again, the judge called him. "Sir, are you Andrés Ricardo Mattías?"

"No, Your Honor. I am Andrés Melardo Mattías. These charges are not mine."

"But the file shows the same birthdate for both names; it has to be you."

"It can't be, Your Honor. I insist on my identity. I am not Andrés Ricardo, but Andrés Melardo."

---

[1] Fictitious name, as are all the names in the narratives of this book.

"Well, that will be up to a jury to decide. Meanwhile, I am going to lock you up. You can pay the bail of $75,000.00 (seventy-five thousand dollars). Take a seat, and don't move unless I say so." Minutes later, a tall, well-built man entered the courtroom.

"Who are you?" asked the judge. "Why are you late?"

"I am sorry, Your Honor. I had car trouble. I am Andrés Ricardo Mattías." A murmur ran through the seated audience. The judge then called Andrés Melardo, and dismissed all charges against him. Andrés Ricardo pled guilty to the charges and was sent to jail.

The Gospel's Good News announced from God's judgment hall to every sinner is rather simple. Jesus Christ appears and pleads guilty in our place. He assumes our identity. He accepts our punishment, suffers it, and dies in my place so that I can be absolved. This is the miracle of divine love, the mystery of grace. The innocent one suffers for the guilty, so that the guilty will be declared innocent. This justice is totally contrary to all human justice. But it is the only way God can condemn all sinners in the person of Christ, and justify them with his perfect life at the same time. In Jesus Christ, we are all condemned, and due to that condemnation in Christ's body, we are exonerated forever of all guilt.

If your mind got lost somewhere in that transaction, read it again because it's about you, and it's a must that you understand it. Scripture says, "God was reconciling the world to himself through Christ, by not counting people's sins against them. He has trusted us with this message of reconciliation" (2 Corinthians 5:19, CEB). All had been foretold by the prophets, and fulfilled by Christ for the least and the greatest of all sinners. "He was pierced because of our rebellions and crushed because of our crimes. He bore the punishment that made us whole; by his wounds we are healed. Like sheep we had all wandered away, each going its own way, but the Lord let fall on him all our crimes" (Isaiah 53:5-6, CEB). When you believe it, you will find out your true name. Your last name is "FORGIVEN." Someone else appeared on your behalf, took all your charges, your offenses before neighbor, self, and God. He took on himself all your illnesses, character defects, and weaknesses so as to give you that new name. Look at your "Absolution Certificate"—ponder, wonder, and worship. Stop and reflect on your new last name. It's yours for eternity.

72

They Left Us All Alone

> "I will not leave you fatherless . . . I will never leave you or let you be alone . . . I am not afraid of anything man can do to me" (John 14:18, MEV; Hebrews 13:5-6, NLV).

"And why don't you go to school?" the attorney asked the thirteen-year-old in the interview room for juvenile detainees.

"It's that I've got to be out there hustling and making some coins, 'ya know what I mean?"

The lawyer led him on: "So how do you make those coins?"

"Hey, back off with the questions, man. Let's say I'm in the delivery business."

"Really? What's your fee?"

"Like a hundred green ones for each baggie with that white powdery stuff. It's more than my old man makes working in the fields all day long, and my old lady ironing clothes for the landowner. I make more a day than both of them together, ha, ha!"

"Do you know that most kids in your business end up in jail?"

"Yeah, but if you kill somebody before you get locked up, you'll get a lot of respect and protection in there."

I saw a brief frown in the lawyer's forehead, but he kept his professional composure. He tried to hide his shudder, and so did I. He wanted to show the minor a bit of jail's cold and cruel reality. "Nicky, I don't doubt it, but before you get all that respect and protection, you know what's going to happen to you?"

"Well, nothing, 'cause my homies are going to protect me!"

The lawyer was not finished. "The first night in the slammer, the homies of the jail's big shot are going to grab you, and one by one, they're gonna rape you. The jail guards disappear for they consider the rape part of your punishment. When you can no longer walk, they'll start kicking you, until finally the guards show up and put you in solitary until you start feeling a little better. Then, if they want to, they throw you once again to the wolves, until one of them claims you as his girlfriend, and then you'll be under his protection. That's all the protection you'll have! Are you getting this?"

Finally, the tough little young man could take it no longer. He began to shake like a leaf in a dry tree, and suddenly broke down in tears, heart-wrenching sobs, until his face was bathed in tears; he could not control his sighs, and his body twisted in grief from side to side. The lawyer approached him and put his arms around his shoulders. "Son, that's the truth, that's how it happens. I'm your attorney; I have to tell you the truth so I can protect you." The boy leaned his head on the lawyer's shoulder and between tears and sighs began to tell his story:

"They left us all alone, left us all alone, we were all alone," he repeated, trembling with anger and pain. "Me and my little sister. I think now they've taken her to a foster home. But back then, my old man left for work before sunrise, and my old lady soon after. They left the tortillas on the stove. I had to dress my five-year-old sister. I was only seven. We'd walk all alone to school, just hand in hand . . . Oh, my little sis . . . when will I see you again?

'At night, my dad would go out drinking with his buddies, or drink out there in the porch. My mom would yell at him to come inside, but he'd get up and slap her around. Then she'd leave for the casino. She'd tell a neighbor, who gave us some supper, to keep an eye on us. But then I would put my little sister to sleep. I'd hold her hand until she fell asleep. I wished so much someone would hold mine. Why did they leave us alone? Why? Why?"

I glanced over at the attorney. He had shed his professionalism, and now his teary-red eyes were just short of breaking out in tears. My handkerchief was already in my hand, and moist in places. "All alone, they left us all alone," repeated the boy, too soon turned into a man. Neither his mom nor his dad had shown up in court for his hearing. "Please sir, give me a dad and a mom. Don't lock me up in

Juve. I don't want to kill anybody. I wanna take care of my little sister. I don't want to be left all alone." The attorney, now forgetting his title, took the boy as if he were his own son and held him in a firm embrace, until the boy's sighs slowly drifted away . . .

This attorney is but a small reflection of Jesus. Because Jesus went to the cross for us, today he is able to tell us: "I will not leave you fatherless . . . I will not leave you nor forsake you." And he tenderly holds us firmly in his eternal embrace.

73

Watson's Admonition . . . Or John's?

> "Whoever believes in him is not condemned, but whoever does not believe stands condemned already because they have not believed in the name of God's one and only Son" (John 3:18, NIV).

Against his lawyer's advice, the defendant decided to take the witness stand. He was charged with Driving Under the Influence for the second time, and causing the death of his passenger. It was late at night. The car he was driving left the road toward the center median where it impacted against a palm tree on the passenger's side. The coroner's report indicated that the passenger had died instantly. The impact against the palm tree had destroyed his cranium. The deceased had been the driver's best friend since infancy. But the charge was murder in the second degree. Murder? Yes, because when he pled guilty to the first DUI charge, he had signed Watson's admonition.

> I understand that being under the influence of alcohol or drugs, or both, impairs my ability to safely operate a motor vehicle. I understand that it is extremely dangerous to human life to drive while under the influence of alcohol or drugs, or both. I understand that if I continue to drive while under the influence of alcohol or drugs, or both, and as a result of my driving, someone is killed, I can be charged with murder.

The defendant testified that no one had read to him that admonition. He alleged that he had signed not knowing what he was signing.

But the evidence against him was his own signature, and the signature of the interpreter certified by the Judicial Council of the state. The jury did not believe his pretext. He was sentenced to life in prison for the murder of his best friend.

Before the judgment seat of God, we get no such admonition for any second offense. Even before the first, we get Isaiah's reality check: "Your whole head is injured, your whole heart afflicted. From the sole of your foot to the top of your head there is no soundness – only wounds and welts and open sores, not cleansed or bandaged or soothed with olive oil" (Isaiah 1:5-6, NIV). Thus, the "wicked person will die for their sin" (Ezekiel 3:18, NIV). That sentence is directed toward the most egregious sinner as well as to the most pious, holy, and loaded with good works media personality, because "all have sinned" has no exceptions. It's about every single person in particular, and all humanity in general. When God takes a scan of the human heart, that is all God sees. We are not only drunk with our second "living under the influence of sin," but many times more. We have also caused the ruin of many more people than we realize. That is why there is a sentence against us condemning us to eternal death.

There is only one exception. A scan of Jesus's heart, the One sent from God as our Substitute, reveals the complete opposite. He is that One of "clean hands and a pure heart, who does not lift up his soul to what is false and does not swear deceitfully" (Psalm 24:4, ESV). And because of this sentence about his life, our own sentence changes. All who believe are accounted just as pure, clean, true, and sane due to no merit of their own, but entirely from his grace. Oh, and there's more. He did sign our own guilty plea declaration, our own failed promise to comply, with all heaven as a witness. And he never forgot it. The pen is Calvary's cross. He was wounded for our transgressions, but our own sentence is lifted by those wounds.

For all who hear this good news, faith is given to believe. Believe that his life is our own, his death is our death, and his resurrection is our future. This is no longer Watson's admonition. It is John's: "He who believes in him is not condemned; he who does not believe is condemned already, because he has not believed in the name of the only begotten Son of God . . . to those who believed in his name, he gave the right to become children of God" (John 3:18, NKJV; John 1:12, NIV). And to all who are not able to believe, he gave power to believe.

74

We Have Spent Our Last Penny

> "We have an Advocate before the Father: Jesus Christ, the Righteous One" (1 John 2:1, EHV).

An attorney of certain prestige said to me, "I need your help in talking to the mother of a defendant." I began to translate. The middle-aged mother wore a fast-food restaurant uniform. Her teary eyes betrayed the pain behind the faint smile in her greeting.

"Your son is about to turn eighteen, but due to the seriousness of the charges, the allegations, he is being treated as an adult."

"Yes, I understand," she replied. The lawyer went on. "There's a new law that favors your son, for it orders such matters as your son's, to go back to Juvenile Court. There, the sentence would not be so serious. Today, I will be asking the judge to apply this law to your son's case, and send him back to Juvenile Hall."

Her eyes became even more tearful when the lawyer turned around to answer someone else's question. The lady touched my arm and asked, "Please tell me, is he a good attorney?"

Not wanting to commit myself, I said, "Madam, I've seen that lawyer deal with very difficult cases."

But she understood that the expression on my face was asking "Why?"

"Sir," she said anxiously, "it's that my husband and I have already paid him $87,000.00 (eighty-seven thousand dollars), and now he's asking for another $20,000.00 (twenty-thousand) to keep the case. My husband and I have given him the last penny of our savings!"

Now it was I with the teary eyes. For a brief moment, I lived the agony she felt for her son. Moments later, I entered the courtroom and went past the section where the custodies await their appearance. I recognized her son. I also overheard him say to his bench mate, "My parents are so lame. They're not doing anything to get me out of here. They don't know what they're doing." The other custodies around him burst out laughing.

The Scriptures declare, "We have an Advocate before the Father: Jesus Christ, the Righteous One" (1 John 2:1, EHV), and he is given to us free of charge. We don't pay a penny, because he himself paid it all. All our life's savings, all the effort of thousands of lifespans - if we could live them - would be insufficient to pay for all Jesus did for us on the cross. He gave his life to forgive our countless sins—and not only our sins, but also the sins of the countless millions of people who have ever lived and are living on the surface of the earth. Just think of that the next time you fly and overlook the cities below with their teeming millions. Even if the millions of all earth's largest cities were to repent and live holy lives before God, that would not be enough to pay for Christ's giving his life on the cross. For he gave us not only his death, but also his perfect life, and then his resurrection. How do you repay someone for arising from the grave and giving life to you? Incredibly, the human heart opposes such great gift of life and forgiveness, so much unmerited grace. It wants some merit for the grace given. At least for repenting, at least for responding with a gift of praise, with the use of talents, such as singing, testifying, preaching, teaching, praying—anything that comes from the self that sees its contributions as meriting (or deserving) a part, be it ever so small, of the gift of grace. But Scripture affirms that all human cooperation, be it ever so sincere, full of love and gratitude, is as "filthy rags" (Isaiah 64:6, NIV). It is Jesus's perfect life as symbolized by his robe of righteousness that must cover every single sinner throughout human history. This free gift of God's grace is ours through faith alone. Our attorney, though owner of heaven's wealth, gave it all away so as to make us rich throughout eternity. It is a *fait accompli*, an accomplished mandate.

Do we need to ask if he's a good attorney? With his resurrection from the dead, he declared that he had already won the case for all humanity. When he rose from the tomb, all humanity arose with him triumphant over death. It's no laughing matter, unless you laugh from sheer joy!

75

They Used Their Children As A Cover

> "So you are no longer a slave, but God's child; and since you are his child, God has made you also an heir" (Galatians 4:7, NIV). "And in [Abraham's] seed Jesus Christ all the families of the earth shall be blessed" (Acts 3:25, NKJV).

"You've been unaware, but you've had a snitch for the past ten years, an informant—one of your clients in your drug trade. Hired by the DEA. He has been informing on you at least once a year."

"And what has he been informing? I've been doing nothing wrong!" This was the conversation between the public defender attorney and his client in custody.

"You and your wife have been using your family, your five children, as a cover-up for your drug trade between the two countries. Up to now, you and your wife have eluded the authorities. The informant says that you bring methamphetamine from the other side of the border. When you cross into this country, your car is full with your five kids and their stuff. But in the trunk, you've got meth hidden among your children's toys and clothes. Even the diapers had cocaine instead of absorbent material. A whole box of diapers so well sealed it looked brand new. Forty diapers containing fifteen pounds of pure, high-quality cocaine. You've had detectives following you. You've gone as far north as Oregon, then Montana, Nevada, and Texas. You've sold large amounts of drugs. Then with a stash of thousands of dollars in cash, you drive back to your country, making it look like you're going on vacation. There you live it up in grand style, beautiful condo, swimming pools, servants, you know what you've got. Your wife has been your accomplice in all your dealings."

"No madam attorney. That is nothing but slander. Never. Just now, okay, I admit this was my first mistake. But my wife, no! She knew nothing at all; she has not an ounce of blame in this."

"Really? You mean to tell me she knew nothing of the ounces of cocaine in the baby powder can?"

After the parents' arrest, all five children were placed in foster homes. They were separated forever from their parents. But, were they really parents for their children? Those parents agreed that they would have lots of kids only to create a good cover for their drug trafficking enterprise. When those kids grow up, what are they going to think when they realize they were only "façade kids?" In other words, "My purpose in life was only to give the appearance of a son, but in fact, I was only a front for my parents' selfish interests! Or, were they just trying to provide for us in the best way possible? But, didn't they know the risks? Didn't they know that if they got caught, that would be the end of our family? Didn't they care?"

Those wounds can only be healed by grasping on to another Father, who has given us all the assurance that we are his children, just because he loves us. That is why with all confidence we can call him "Our Father who are in heaven." He has proven that we are his dearly loved children when the Son offered to give his life for us. The blood of Christ shed on the cross for all the families of the earth attracts us and brings us to him as one family of beloved children. Humanity is destroying itself because it has lost its sense of belonging as one family with one purpose: to be loved by him. Entire countries and world powers only use their citizens as "fronts" to pursue their selfish goals. Not so with our heavenly Father. Scripture tells us, "So you are no longer a slave ["*a front*"], but God's child; and since you are his child, God has made you also an heir" (Galatians 4:7, NIV). This is a promise fulfilled to humanity. In Christ shall be blessed all the families of the earth (Acts 3:25). Neither our past nor our present matters; we are no one's "front." We are children freed and blessed forever! The only way to redeem our families is to claim for them the salvation obtained through Christ by faith alone. "Believe in the Lord Jesus, and you will be saved, you and your household!" (Acts 16:31, LEB).

76

I Forgot I Was Married

> "For Christ also suffered once for sins, the righteous for the unrighteous, to bring you to God" (1 Peter 3:18, NIV). "What will you gain, if you own the whole world but destroy yourself? What would you give to get back your soul?" (Matthew 16:26, CEV).

The couple was appearing in Family Law. The husband was requesting a divorce. That was not unusual. Yet, there was something strange to this case. The couple had taken a seat in the Petitioner's side of the table. Their shoulders touched gently as they waited. In most divorce cases, each takes a seat at opposite sides of the table. The advanced age of the couple was also out of the ordinary. The man appeared to be at least seventy years old due to the white canopy of his hair, and his face was already marked by numerous wrinkles signed by each passing year. The woman was not far behind. The judge immediately took note. "Well, neither of you look all bitter and mad, as is usual here. Are you sure you want a divorce?"

The woman answered first. "No, Your Honor, but he says it's for the best."

"Well," replied the judge. "I am not here to do marriage therapy. But sir, tell me, what's going on?"

"You see, Your Honor, I married her a few years ago. Yes, we still love each other, but it's a matter of my conscience. I need a divorce so that God will forgive me."

"Stop right there," said the judge. "I'm not here to pass judgment on divine proceedings," added the judge in good humor.

"Your Honor, it's that when I married her, I forgot that I was still married in my home country."

To which the judge retorted, "But where is the other woman now? Is she here to contest the divorce?"

"She's dead, Your Honor."

The judge had a powerful reply: "In that case, sir, God has also forgotten that you were married. I deny your divorce petition. Enjoy all the years God may still give you together!"

As they left the courtroom, the couple suddenly shed decades of their age. They seemed to be dancing in step, arm in arm, as if they were dancing on their wedding day. I overheard the judge commenting out loud: "But the marriage vow is only 'unto death do us part.'"

But then he continued, commenting to his staff that he had read the entire file. The other woman had also remarried in her own country and died some years after. "The problem is that some sects teach that if you married someone else while already married, regardless of the reason, you have to pay for such a sin, for they consider it a sin. You no longer have the right to intimate love with anyone else. Only if you divorce the second spouse, and live alone, God is able to forgive you. You have to pay for your own sins."

Obviously, the judge did not consent to that idea. But that is what the world and many faiths still teach: "You have to pay for your own sins; otherwise, you will not be justified before God!" But how different is the teaching of Scripture: "For Christ also suffered once for sins, the righteous for the unrighteous, to bring you to God" (1 Peter 3:18, NIV). "What will you gain, if you own the whole world but destroy yourself? What would you give to get back your soul?" (Matthew 16:26, CEV). Our sins are so great and perverse that there is no way for us to square off our account with God. That was only done in Christ's holy being: the crucified God on the cross, squaring off our account with God. There all guilt was declared null and void, and there he fulfilled his marriage vow to love us unto death and beyond into eternal life.

77

Death Sentence In The Pocket

> "He canceled out every legal violation we had on our record and the old arrest warrant that stood to indict us. He erased it all—our sins, our stained soul—he deleted it all and they cannot be retrieved!" (Colossians 2:14, TPT).

"Look, sir," she pleaded with her client. "You're running a huge risk taking that document with you into jail. Your cell is not secure. There's no place you can hide it there."

"Don't worry. I know that as my attorney you worry about me, but I know how to watch out for myself."

"Still, sir, I don't recommend it," continued the attorney. "The accusations against you are extremely serious. That document contains the charges and allegations against you. The district attorney accuses you of sexually abusing a minor under twelve years old, during three long years for that little girl. Do you know what the other custodies are going to do to you when they find out the charges against you?"

"Madam, don't worry about me."

"Alright, I want to be as clear as possible with you, sir. You are going to get raped in jail, and no one is going to save you!"

"No. madam, you don't know how things are in there. I'm protected. I have my buddies, my homies."

"Sir, even the homies have been known to turn against sexual abusers of minors."

But he responded, "I know what I'm doing. Besides, it's my right to have those documents. Hand me my copy."

"Sir, those documents describe explicitly what you did to that little girl when she was nine years old. The other custodies are going to do the same to you, and worse. Don't you understand?"

"I know how to take care of myself," he said with a sly smile

"Let me put it another way," replied the attorney once again. "They're going to kill you!"

"Give me those docs, lady; I insist on my rights." As she folded the documents and placed them in his shirt pocket, she whispered so he could hear her, "You're taking your death sentence in your pocket."

As the bailiff led him out of the courtroom, he whispered to her, "This year, we've taken two of them out in body bags for the same reason."

This man had also insisted on his innocence, but why take your death sentence in your pocket? His pretext was that he would go to the jail library. There he'd research how to defend himself from all those false allegations, because he had done nothing wrong. Everything was slander and revenge. But in matters of sexual abuse of minors, the inmates neither wait nor forgive. They take the accused as guilty, and they are relentless. They will either torture or kill the suspects. There is little the bailiffs and guards can do to prevent it, even less to stop it. This man did not pay attention to his attorney. "I know how to take care of myself; I insist on my rights. I know what I'm doing; I know how to defend myself. I want to keep the document that accuses me of terrible crimes."

Scripture tells us that we too have a document against us, with much worse information. It contains all the legal demands of God's law, and how we have broken each one—in explicit detail. It is the worst document that we could ever keep in our possession. The evil in the world recognizes when we still live under its accusations. They recognize the fear and the anxiety we experience, and only seek to add to its threats and terrors. That is why long ago, on the cross of Calvary, Jesus took that document, changed our name to his name, and then nailed it to the cross. By that single act, he saved us from ever having in our possession the history of all that accused us before God. He then transferred over to our file in heaven the entire record of his life, his record of constant love toward self, neighbor, and God. It is fixed in our heavenly record as if we had lived the life of Christ. The Passion Translation of Colossians 2:14 puts it this way:

"He canceled out every legal violation we had on our record and the old arrest warrant that stood to indict us. He erased it all—our sins, our stained soul—he deleted it all and they cannot be retrieved! Everything we once were in Adam has been placed onto his cross and nailed permanently there as a public display of cancellation" (Colossians 2:14, TPT).

So we are free, not only of the document that accused us, but also from the jail and the cell that held us in bondage. Again, the Passion Translation colorfully gives us a picture of our freedom and Christ's power in subduing everything that ever held us captive:

"Then Jesus made a public spectacle of all the powers and principalities of darkness, stripping away from them every weapon and all their spiritual authority and power to accuse us. And by the power of the cross, Jesus led them around as prisoners in a procession of triumph. He was not their prisoner; they were his!" (Colossians 2:15, TPT).

But even in that extreme scenario, at the cross God set all captives free, and when "the Son makes you free, you are truly free" (John 8:36, NLT). And in that freedom, we worship!

78

An Entire Love Story In One Tear

> "He will wipe away every tear from their eyes, and death shall be no more, neither shall there be mourning, nor crying, nor pain anymore, for the former things have passed away" (Revelation 21:4, ESV).

First, the judge addressed the husband, seated to the left of the table, indicating he was the petitioner of the divorce. "Sir, this is your divorce petition. Do you still wish to go ahead with the petition?" "Yes, Your Honor," he answered firmly and deliberately. "Is your marriage so broken that there is no way to repair it?" "That is so, Your Honor." "Is there something the court can offer, as in therapy, that could prevent this divorce?" "No, Your Honor, thank you."

Then the judge addressed the wife with the same questions. Her answers were the same as the husband's. She agreed with the petition, there was no hope for the marriage, and there was no way to repair it. "Then," continued the judge, "by the power vested in me by this State, I grant your divorce petition. From now on, both of you are restored to your status as single persons." As I translated the words of the judge, something caught my eye to the right, where the lady was seated. It was a reflection of light, which lasted for an instant. Then I saw it. A tiny tear had formed in the lady's left eye. The eye reddened briefly, the tear reflected a light from a nearby lamp, and the reflection disappeared as quickly as it had come. There was just a tinge of pink left in the eye. The tear had reabsorbed completely.

Out in the hallway, the woman apologized. "Excuse me, sir, I was on the verge of tears."

"Yes, madam, but it was only a tiny tear."

"Oh sir, it may have seemed tiny, but all our fifteen years of marriage were in that tear."

A funeral is much like a divorce. But death's good-bye is definitive. There are many divorcees who remarry, even back to their former spouses. Not so with death. The separation is final. When Lazarus died, his sisters called Jesus, who was their close friend. But they chided him, "If you had been here, our brother would not have died." When Jesus finally came, he asked to be taken to the tomb. A large group of mourners had gathered, and they all followed him to the graveside. Once there, Jesus heard the cry and saw the tears of all humanity; he felt how death had overwhelmed his creation because they had separated from him, the fountain of life. He felt every moment of grief caused by death to the human family.

All of humanity's history with life, sin, and death was wrapped together in that moment. Yet the love and life of God was also present in the person of Jesus, the Creator. The pain of death and the triumph of life seemed to overwhelm him, and "Jesus wept" (John 11:35, ESV). The entire history of God's love for us was gathered together in those tears. But through the lenses of those tears, Jesus saw you and me. He saw our entire history, and even so, loved us, and that love wept for us. His tears were not in vain, for not long after they became drops of blood shed to give us pardon and life. He took our place on the cross, and with the Word of forgiveness on his lips, he loved us to the end. In the coming life, our tears will join with his, but then they will be tears of joy, because his life and his love for us will have no end! But even those tears will be short lived, because "He will wipe away every tear from their eyes, and death shall be no more, neither shall there be mourning, nor crying, nor pain anymore, for the former things have passed away" (Revelation 21:4, ESV).

79

Let's Take Daddy His Birthday Present

> "But he was being punished for what we did. He was crushed because of our guilt. He took the punishment we deserved, and this brought us peace. We were healed because of his pain" (Isaiah 53:5, ERV).

When the detectives arrived, the two mothers were taking from the trunks of their cars, what seemed to be grocery bags. The women quickly walked through the open garage door, and came back for more. Two boys had emerged from the cars and were playing innocently in the front yard with some toy cars. It seemed like a peaceful scene in any suburban setting. The detectives had been taking pictures from a van parked at some distance. At an agreed moment, they left the van and walked toward the two women. They were dressed in civilian clothes. But after a brief greeting, they displayed their DEA badges, and announced they had a search warrant for the property and all its occupants. The women ran toward their children, took them by the hand and ran for their cars. But there was another officer standing by each vehicle. Then, several patrol cars surrounded and blocked the driveway. A couple of women agents took charge of the children while their mothers were read their rights and handcuffed. In the driveway, the detectives were already taking pictures of grocery bags tucked away in the washer and dryer. There were six bags altogether, each containing five bricks of high-quality cocaine, weighing just over two pounds. Thirty bricks altogether, with a street value of $1,000,000.00 (one million dollars)! Days later, handcuffed, dressed in jail blues; they were in court for their arraignment. The attorneys explained to them that they were facing charges for storage, transport, and sales of cocaine. But further, they were facing charges of child neglect for risking the lives of their two children, who would remain in foster homes under the custody of the court. "But what do the kids have to do with any of this? They've done nothing wrong," said one of the mothers. "The only thing we told them is that we were taking daddy his birthday presents."

Incidents like these leave one speechless. But the law does not lack for words. The women were facing fifteen years of jail each, and the loss of parental rights over their children. We too have our words: Insolence! The nerve! Infamy! Perversity! Abuse! There are others perhaps more fitting, but they won't fit here. Mothers like this bring out our feelings of great indignation. We repudiate their actions. We want to join in the accusations, and follow through to the sentencing and punishment of these women who don't deserve the name of mothers!

Even so, we hear the voice from the heavenly courtroom: "He who is without sin among you, let him throw the first stone" (John 8:7, WEB). It seems incredible, but everything bad we would wish on these mothers, and the worst punishment that could be meted to them, has already fallen on the pure and innocent body of Christ. None of the bodies, minds, or spirits of these mothers could withstand the punishment for the infamy they committed against their children, and against society, and for the brashness of their acts. But of Jesus, the Scripture says, "You have prepared a body for me" (Hebrews 10:5, ERV). And it was so. His holy being—spirt, body, mind, and soul—were prepared to carry the penalty that no human being could ever bear. That is why Scripture also says, "By his wounds we were healed" (Isaiah 53:5, NABRE). Could it be there's someone else hiding any such bricks of sins in their soul's garage? But that body of Christ also carried all your soul's bricks . . . and mine, to heal us and love us forever!

80

Me Too, Me, Too

> "Blessed be the God and Father of our Lord Jesus Christ, who has blessed us with every spiritual blessing in the heavenly places in Christ, just as He chose us in Him before the foundation of the world, that we should be holy and without blame before Him in love, having predestined us to adoption as sons by Jesus Christ to Himself, according to the good pleasure of His will, to the praise of the glory of His grace, by which He made us accepted in the Beloved. In Him we have redemption through His blood, the forgiveness of sins, according to the riches of His grace" (Ephesians 1:3-7, NKJV).

The bailiff announced the beginning of the proceedings. "Your Honor, we're ready to begin the adoption ceremony!" First through the door was a six-year-old boy, wearing colored striped pants, and a Superman shirt with his hands in his pockets, looking all around. Behind him was a seven-year-old girl wearing a little dress with flowers and butterflies; it seemed she floated above the floor. Next in line entered a two-year-old girl dressed in a white embroidered dress with a rebellious little white lace on her hair that her sister was trying to keep in place. Behind entered the adoptive parents. Certainly, love had brought them to adopt these three children, all from different parents. Last to enter was a woman with an orphanage stamped uniform. Holding tightly to the caretaker's hand was a three-year-old boy. However, he was not in the group to be adopted.

It seemed the only thing he wore were his great big coffee-colored eyes that took in everything and everyone all around. Throughout the ceremony, I noticed that the boy would timidly raise his hand above the bench in front. Soon the adoption ceremony was over, and the judge invited all the children and the adoptive parents to take a picture with him at the judge's bench. The boy with the Superman shirt, posed with the judge's gavel in hand. All the others gathered around the judge and their new parents. After the picture, the bailiff handed out all types of stuffed toy animals to the adoptees, and suddenly the judge's bench turned into a hugging and celebrating podium. In the audience, the three-year-old boy, who had not lost a detail, was now boldly waving his hands back and forth. The judge finally noted and asked him, "And you, young man, what do you want?"

"Me too, me too, me too!" he cried out.

The judge invited him to come forward, gave him a big bear hug, covered him with his judicial robe, gave him a teddy bear, and promised that very soon he too would have a new family.

In Bethlehem's manger, it was baby Jesus waving his hands on behalf of all humanity, crying out, "Me too, me too, me too!" He had to do it on our behalf, because our proud heart thinks we can grow up by ourselves just fine. We think all we need in this life is the proper use of our reason—we prefer to call it common sense—and with that we'll grow up nice and tall. But he saw our desolating loneliness, for all of us withdraw into shells of our own making. We even push our own families aside and afar. We don various masks to pretend we are happy, satisfied, even keeled. But inside, we wave our hands in the silence of our lonely hearts, "Me too, me too!" Therefore, "Blessed be the God and Father of our Lord Jesus Christ, who has blessed us with every spiritual blessing in the heavenly places in Christ, just as He chose us in Him before the foundation of the world, that we should be holy and without blame before Him in love, having predestined us to adoption as sons by Jesus Christ to Himself, according to the good pleasure of His will, to the praise of the glory of His grace, by which He made us accepted in the Beloved. In Him we have redemption through His blood, the forgiveness of sins, according to the riches of His grace" (Ephesians 1:3-7, NKJV). And we are even invited to come up to the Judge's bench where he gives us the most loving hug we've ever had, and then ushers us to feast with the entire family of the universe! There's no reason for anyone to be left behind. Through Christ's sacrifice, God's loving wish for the entire human family has come true, "You too, you too!"

81

You've Given Me Nothing!

> "Consequently, just as one offense resulted in condemnation for everyone, so one act of righteousness results in justification and life for everyone. For just as through one man's disobedience many people were made sinners, so also through one man's obedience many people will be made righteous." (Romans 5:18-19, ISV).

"I'm sorry to remind you, madam, but today's hearing will not be to your liking. Most likely, the Judge will rule that you have lost your parental rights over your boy."

"And what does that mean?" replied the young mother.

"I've explained it to you many times," continued the attorney. "The judge gave you eighteen months to finish your parenting classes, your drug rehabilitation program, and your therapy sessions with your boy. You have done nothing! You've run out of chances. Today you will lose your legal rights as a mother. Your son's foster parents will assume the first right of adoption."

The mother's calm facial expression suddenly changed to surprise, anger, and pain, and with great sobs and cries, she hid her face between her hands. "Please ask the judge for one more chance. I know she will hear you; I plead with you, don't take my son away from me."

"But you've given me nothing with which to plead. You haven't gone to one single class, no drug rehab, and no therapies with your son. You've even given dirty drug tests. But, could you even tell me one reason why you didn't go to the parenting classes?"

"It's that at that time, it's too hot, I don't have a ride, I don't like taking the bus, and I don't have a car."

Moments later, the judge rolled her eyes when she heard those excuses and would not hear any further arguments. Immediately, she announced the date for the adoption hearing. She also added, "Your boy doesn't even want to go back with you; he says he is doing just fine with his foster parents. They will soon adopt him as their own son." No words can describe the pain and horror of that mother when she realized she had lost her son forever.

Our first parents took a similar decision. When they had the opportunity to become the parents of an entire race of beings made in God's image, they gave way to their greed to become as God. They gave up their parental rights over the human race in exchange for seeking positions and titles for which they had not been created. They sought to be as God their creator, when they were only creatures. But parents they were. Their legacy to the human race was their greed. They lost their parental rights to what could have been an entire race of creative, loving people, perfectly in tune with their Creator.

But not all was lost. The Judge of the universe gave us a new father, a second Adam. Yes! Jesus Christ himself is also our new and better Adam. All humanity has been created once again, but in him. "Consequently, just as one offense resulted in condemnation for everyone, so one act of righteousness results in justification and life for everyone. For just as through one man's disobedience many people were made sinners, so also through one man's obedience many people will be made righteous." (Romans 5:18-19, ISV). Jesus is our new creation, and that's how he redeemed us, in the perfection of his humanity, and not in our own. Our own is nothing but the residue of the first Adam's humanity. It is worthless before God. But we stand before God in Christ's perfect humanity. And by faith in his singular life of righteousness, we are forever declared righteous before God!

82

Sexual Predator In The Middle of Mass?

> "Who will bring any charge against those whom God has chosen? It is God who justifies. Who then is the one who condemns? No one. Christ Jesus who died—more than that, who was raised to life—is at the right hand of God and is also interceding for us" (Romans 8:33-34, NIV).

"Your Honor, I need a Stay-away order from this woman because she creates a scene when she sees me at mass."

"Go ahead, sir. Explain your petition."

"Your Honor, right in the middle of mass, she stands up, and in front of everyone, including children, she points at me and shouts, 'That man is a sexual predator, a pedophile, take a good look at him, watch out for that predator.' That is quite embarrassing because my own children hear it; she's defaming me in public."

"And what do you have to say about those claims, madam?"

"Your Honor, it's that you already gave me a restraining order on that pervert, because that rapist was harassing me sexually."

To which the judge replied, "Is it true that children hear all your shouting?"

"Frankly, Your Honor, I don't know. What I want is for that man not to set foot at mass when I'm there."

The story began to emerge through the testimony of several witnesses. The petitioner was married, and so was the respondent. But both had been involved in a sultry love affair with each other. The woman's husband was demanding she get a restraining order against her previous lover if he was "ever going to forgive her." The petitioner confessed to the affair, but that he no longer wanted anything to do with the woman. Yet she stalked him in the shopping centers, at church, at school, always shouting the same allegations in public and in front of children.

The judge admonished the woman that she ran the risk of getting sued for defamation of character, and it was not proper for children to be hearing those allegations shouted in public. He further told her that the man's file did not contain any allegations of sexual harassment anywhere. If she at any moment felt attacked by anyone, and had witnesses to corroborate the aggression, she could call the police. "It's unjust for you, madam, to slander this man in public for acts he has not committed," concluded the judge. However, as the hearing ended, one had the feeling that there were other chapters yet to be written in that story.

The slander against Jesus also took place in the middle of religious services and by apparently religious people and their leaders. "He sets himself up as God," they would claim. "He said he would destroy this temple and rebuild it in three days! He teaches against the laws of our ancestors. He does not allow us to stone adulterers, fornicators, and Sabbath breakers! He violates the law of Moses. He doesn't keep the Sabbath. He must be stoned according to the law!" The worst slander, the allegations against him were all worthy of death, in the midst of religious services, in the temple itself, and by the leading religious authorities. And even though the law itself prohibited such slander ("Thou shall not bear false witness"), it was necessary for him to be singled out, accused, and condemned as a sinner. Why? So that we would not be singled out, accused, and condemned as sinners. For he carried our sins on his own body (1 Peter 2:24), to such an extent that he became sin for the totality of all inhuman humanity. He was condemned in our place. When he was crucified, we were crucified; when he was buried, we were buried; when he resurrected, we arose with him.

"Who will bring any charge against those whom God has chosen? It is God who justifies. Who then is the one who condemns? No one. Christ Jesus who died—more than that, who was raised to life—is at the right hand of God and is also interceding for us" (Romans 8:33-34, NIV).

And that reality describes both the end, and the beginning of our story!

www.ingramcontent.com/pod-product-compliance
Lightning Source LLC
LaVergne TN
LVHW091113080826
845145LV00008B/1902

* 9 7 8 1 9 5 6 6 5 8 0 6 4 *